Enjoy!

your Secret Pal

2009

FAVORITE BRAND NAME™
BEST-LOVED
Entertaining

Publications International, Ltd.

Favorite Brand Name Recipes at www.fbnr.com

Pictured on the front cover: Glazed Cornish Hens *(page 78).*
Pictured on the jacket flaps: Mini Marinated Beef Skewers *(page 8)* and Wild Rice, Cranberry and Apple Stuffing *(page 122).*
Pictured on the back cover *(left to right):* Cornmeal Pancakes with Blueberries *(page 172),* Santa Fe BBQ Ranch Salad *(page 54)* and Classic Banana Cake *(page 200).*

ISBN-13: 978-1-4127-2634-4
ISBN-10: 1-4127-2634-4

Library of Congress Control Number: 2007925183

Manufactured in China.

8 7 6 5 4 3 2 1

Microwave Cooking: Microwave ovens vary in wattage. Use the cooking times as guidelines and check for doneness before adding more time.

Preparation/Cooking Times: Preparation times are based on the approximate amount of time required to assemble the recipe before cooking, baking, chilling or serving. These times include preparation steps such as measuring, chopping and mixing. The fact that some preparations and cooking can be done simultaneously is taken into account. Preparation of optional ingredients and serving suggestions is not included.

Table of
CONTENTS

All-Occasion APPETIZERS

Festive Taco Cups (page 24)

Original Buffalo Chicken Wings (page 14)

Baked Brie (page 6)

Easy Spinach Appetizer

2 tablespoons butter

3 eggs

1 cup all-purpose flour

1 cup milk

1 teaspoon baking powder

1 teaspoon salt

2 packages (10 ounces each) frozen chopped spinach, thawed and well drained

4 cups (16 ounces) shredded Monterey Jack cheese

½ cup diced red bell pepper

1. Preheat oven to 350°F. Melt butter in 13×9-inch baking pan.

2. Beat eggs in medium bowl. Add milk, flour, baking powder and salt; beat until well blended. Stir in spinach, cheese and bell pepper; mix well. Spread mixture in pan.

3. Bake 40 to 45 minutes or until set. Let stand 10 minutes; cut into triangles or squares to serve.   *Makes 2 to 4 dozen pieces*

TIP: This delicious appetizer can also be made ahead, frozen and reheated. After baking, cool completely and cut into squares. Transfer the squares to a baking sheet; place it in the freezer until the squares are frozen solid. Transfer to a large resealable food storage bag. To serve, reheat the squares in a preheated 325°F oven for 15 minutes.

Baked Brie

½ pound Brie cheese, rind removed

¼ cup chopped pecans

¼ cup KARO® Dark Corn Syrup

1. Preheat oven to 350°F. Place cheese in shallow oven-safe serving dish. Top with pecans and corn syrup.

2. Bake 8 to 10 minutes or until cheese is almost melted. Serve warm with plain crackers or melba toast.   *Makes 8 servings*

Easy Spinach Appetizer

Mini Marinated Beef Skewers

1 boneless beef top sirloin steak (about 1 pound)

2 tablespoons dry sherry

2 tablespoons soy sauce

1 tablespoon dark sesame oil

2 cloves garlic, minced

18 cherry tomatoes

1. Cut beef crosswise into ⅛-inch slices. Place in large resealable food storage bag. Combine sherry, soy sauce, sesame oil and garlic in small bowl; pour over beef. Seal bag; turn to coat. Marinate in refrigerator at least 30 minutes or up to 2 hours. Soak 18 (6-inch) wooden skewers in water 20 minutes.

2. Preheat broiler. Drain beef; discard marinade. Weave beef accordion style onto skewers. Place on rack of broiler pan.

3. Broil, 4 to 5 inches from heat, 4 minutes. Turn skewers over; broil 4 minutes or until beef is barely pink in center. Garnish each skewer with one cherry tomato. Serve warm or at room temperature. *Makes 18 appetizers*

Cocktail Wraps

16 thin strips Cheddar cheese*

16 HILLSHIRE FARM® Lit'l Smokies, scored lengthwise

1 can (8 ounces) refrigerated crescent roll dough

1 egg, beaten *or* 1 tablespoon milk

Mustard

Or substitute Swiss, taco-flavored or other variety of cheese.

Preheat oven to 400°F.

Place 1 strip cheese inside score of each Lit'l Smokie. Separate dough into 8 triangles; cut each lengthwise into halves to make 16 triangles. Place 1 link on wide end of 1 dough triangle; roll up. Repeat with remaining links and dough triangles. Place links on baking sheet. Brush dough with egg. Bake 10 to 15 minutes.

Serve hot with mustard. *Makes 16 hors d'oeuvres*

Mini Marinated Beef Skewers

Easy Cheesy Artichoke & Spinach Bread

1 can (14 ounces) artichoke hearts, drained and chopped

1 package (10 ounces) frozen chopped spinach or chopped broccoli, thawed and squeezed dry

1 cup HELLMANN'S® or BEST FOODS® Real Mayonnaise

1 cup grated Parmesan cheese

1 clove garlic, finely chopped *or* ¼ teaspoon LAWRY'S® Garlic Powder with Parsley (optional)

1 loaf French or Italian bread (about 16 inches long), halved lengthwise

1. Preheat oven to 350°F.

2. In small bowl, combine all ingredients except bread; evenly spread on bread. Bake 12 minutes or until golden and heated through.   *Makes 8 servings*

Prep Time: 10 minutes
Cook Time: 12 minutes

Hot & Sweet Deviled Eggs

6 hard-cooked eggs, peeled and halved lengthwise

4 to 5 tablespoons mayonnaise

¼ teaspoon curry powder

¼ teaspoon black pepper

⅛ teaspoon salt

Dash paprika

1 teaspoon minced fresh chives

¼ cup sweetened dried cherries, finely chopped

Additional fresh chives or green onions (optional)

1. Scoop egg yolks into medium bowl; reserve whites. Mash yolks with mayonnaise until creamy. Stir in curry powder, pepper, salt and paprika; mix well. Stir in chives and cherries.

2. Spoon yolk mixture into egg whites. Garnish with additional chives.   *Makes 6 servings*

Easy Cheesy Artichoke & Spinach Bread

Olive Tapenade Dip

1½ **cups (10-ounce jar) pitted kalamata olives**

3 **tablespoons olive oil**

3 **tablespoons *French's*® Spicy Brown Mustard**

1 **tablespoon minced fresh rosemary leaves *or* 1 teaspoon dried rosemary leaves**

1 **teaspoon minced garlic**

1. Place all ingredients in food processor. Process until puréed.

2. Serve with vegetable crudités or pita chips.   *Makes 4 (¼-cup) servings*

TIP: To pit olives, place in resealable food storage bag. Gently tap with wooden mallet or rolling pin until olives split open. Remove pits.

Crisp Tortellini Bites

½ **cup plain dry bread crumbs**

¼ **cup grated Parmesan cheese**

2 **teaspoons HERB-OX® chicken flavored bouillon**

¼ **teaspoon garlic powder**

½ **cup sour cream**

2 **tablespoons milk**

1 **(9-ounce) package refrigerated cheese filled tortellini**

Warm pizza sauce or marinara sauce, for dipping

Heat oven to 400°F. In small bowl, combine bread crumbs, Parmesan cheese, bouillon and garlic powder. In another small bowl, combine sour cream and milk. Dip tortellini in sour cream mixture, then in bread crumbs; coat evenly. Place tortellini on baking sheet. Bake 10 to 12 minutes or until crisp and golden brown, turning once. Serve immediately with warm pizza or marinara sauce.   *Makes 8 servings*

TIP: The bouillon mixture makes a great coating for chicken fingers or mild fish.

Prep Time: 15 minutes
Total Time: 30 minutes

Olive Tapenade Dip

Original Buffalo Chicken Wings

Zesty Blue Cheese Dip (recipe follows)

2½ **pounds chicken wings, split and tips discarded**

½ **cup** *Frank's® RedHot®* **Original Cayenne Pepper Sauce (or to taste)**

⅓ **cup butter or margarine, melted**

Celery sticks

1. Prepare Zesty Blue Cheese Dip.

2. Deep fry* wings at 400°F 12 minutes or until crisp and no longer pink; drain.

3. Combine *Frank's RedHot* Sauce and butter in large bowl. Add wings to sauce; toss to coat evenly. Serve with Zesty Blue Cheese Dip and celery.

Makes 24 to 30 individual pieces

Or, prepare wings using one of the cooking methods below. Add wings to sauce; toss well to coat completely.

TO BAKE: Place wings in a single layer on rack in foil-lined roasting pan. Bake at 425°F 1 hour or until crisp and no longer pink, turning halfway through baking time.

TO BROIL: Place wings in a single layer on rack in foil-lined roasting pan. Broil 6 inches from heat 15 to 20 minutes or until crisp and no longer pink, turning once.

TO GRILL: Place wings on an oiled grid. Grill, over medium heat, 30 to 40 minutes or until crisp and no longer pink, turning often.

Zesty Blue Cheese Dip

½ **cup blue cheese salad dressing**

¼ **cup sour cream**

2 **teaspoons** *Frank's® RedHot®* **Original Cayenne Pepper Sauce**

Combine all ingredients in medium serving bowl; mix well. Garnish with crumbled blue cheese, if desired.

Makes ¾ cup dip

Original Buffalo Chicken Wings

Chili Cashews

1 tablespoon vegetable oil

2 teaspoons chili powder

1 teaspoon ground cumin

½ teaspoon granulated sugar

½ teaspoon red pepper flakes

2 cups roasted, salted whole cashews (about 9 ounces)

1. Preheat oven to 350°F. Line baking sheet with aluminum foil.

2. Combine oil, chili powder, cumin, sugar and red pepper flakes in medium bowl. Add nuts, stirring to coat. Transfer mixture to prepared baking sheet and spread in single layer. Bake 8 to 10 minutes or until golden, stirring once or twice.

3. Cool completely on baking sheet. Store in airtight container.   *Makes 2 cups*

Garlic Bean Dip

4 cloves garlic

1 can (about 15 ounces) pinto or black beans, rinsed and drained

¼ cup pimiento-stuffed green olives

4½ teaspoons lemon juice

½ teaspoon ground cumin

Assorted fresh vegetables and crackers

1. Place garlic in food processor; process until minced. Add beans, olives, lemon juice and cumin; process until well blended but not entirely smooth.

2. Serve with vegetables and crackers.   *Makes about 1½ cups*

TIP: To save time, buy fresh vegetables, such as carrots and celery, already cut up from the produce section of the supermarket.

Chili Cashews

Ginger Plum Spareribs

  1 jar (10 ounces) damson plum preserves or apple jelly

  ⅓ cup KARO® Light or Dark Corn Syrup

  ⅓ cup soy sauce

  ¼ cup chopped green onions

  2 cloves garlic, minced

  2 teaspoons ground ginger

  2 pounds pork spareribs, trimmed, cut into serving pieces

1. In small saucepan combine preserves, corn syrup, soy sauce, green onions, garlic and ginger. Stirring constantly, cook over medium heat until melted and smooth.

2. Pour into 11×7×2-inch baking dish. Add ribs, turning to coat. Cover; refrigerate several hours or overnight, turning once.

3. Remove ribs from marinade; place on rack in shallow baking pan.

4. Bake in 350°F oven about 1 hour or until tender, turning occasionally and basting with marinade.   *Makes about 20 servings*

GINGER PLUM CHICKEN WINGS: Omit spareribs. Follow recipe for Ginger Plum Spareribs, using 2½ pounds chicken wings, separated at the joints (tips discarded). Bake 45 minutes, basting with marinade during last 30 minutes.

Hot Crab-Cheddar Spread

  1 (8-ounce) container crabmeat, drained and shredded

  8 ounces CABOT® Mild or Sharp Cheddar, grated (about 2 cups)

  ½ cup mayonnaise

  ¼ teaspoon Worcestershire sauce

1. Preheat oven to 350°F.

2. In medium bowl, mix together all ingredients thoroughly. Transfer to small (1-quart) baking dish. Bake for 25 to 35 minutes or until lightly browned on top and bubbling at edges. Serve with crackers or bread toasts.   *Makes 8 to 10 servings*

Ginger Plum Spareribs

Crostini with Lemony Pesto

1 French baguette (about 4 ounces)
3 tablespoons prepared pesto
½ teaspoon lemon juice
½ cup chopped plum tomato

1. Preheat oven to 350°F.

2. Cut baguette crosswise into 16 slices; arrange on baking sheet. Bake 11 to 12 minutes or until bread begins to brown. Cool completely.

3. Meanwhile, combine pesto and lemon juice in small bowl. Spread each bread slice with ½ teaspoon pesto mixture. Top with tomato. Serve immediately.   *Makes 8 servings*

Honey Holiday Wraps

1 package frozen puff pastry sheets, thawed according to package directions
1 egg, beaten
¼ cup Honey Mustard Sauce (recipe follows)
½ pound JENNIE-O TURKEY STORE® Deli Homestyle Honey Cured Turkey Breast, thinly sliced and finely diced
¼ cup walnuts, toasted and chopped
4 ounces Brie cheese, cut into 18 pieces

Preheat oven to 375°F. Remove pastry sheets from package and cut each into 9 squares. Brush pastry squares with beaten egg and drizzle lightly with Honey Mustard Sauce. Toss diced turkey with walnuts. Spoon about 1 teaspoon turkey mixture in center of each pastry square. Top with piece of Brie; fold pastry over diagonally to form triangle and press edges to seal. Pinch together two corners on folded edge of pastry to form tortellini shape; place on baking sheet. Bake at 375°F degrees for 15 to 18 minutes. Cool slightly before serving. Serve with additional Honey Mustard Sauce, if desired.   *Makes 18 wraps*

HONEY MUSTARD SAUCE: Combine 2 tablespoons Dijon mustard and 2 tablespoons honey. Makes ¼ cup.

VARIATIONS: Any variety of JENNIE-O TURKEY STORE® turkey or chicken breast can be used in this recipe. Try apple butter or pesto sauce instead of honey mustard.

Crostini with Lemony Pesto

Brie Bites

  1 package (17½ ounces) frozen puff pastry sheets, thawed
  ¼ cup apricot preserves or red pepper jelly
  1 (5-inch) brie round, cut into 32 chunks

1. Preheat oven to 400°F. Cut each puff pastry sheet into 16 squares.

2. Spread ½ teaspoon apricot preserves on each square. Place cube of brie on one side of square and fold over opposite edge of pastry. Press with tines of fork to seal completely. Place 1 inch apart on ungreased baking sheets.

3. Bake 10 to 13 minutes or until pastry is light golden brown.   *Makes 32 appetizers*

Creamy Hot Artichoke Dip

  1 can (14 ounces) artichoke hearts, drained and chopped
  1 cup HELLMANN'S® or BEST FOODS® Real Mayonnaise
  1 cup grated Parmesan cheese (about 4 ounces)
  1 clove garlic, finely chopped *or* ¼ teaspoon LAWRY'S® Garlic Powder With Parsley
     (optional)

1. Preheat oven to 350°F.

2. In 1-quart casserole, combine all ingredients. Bake, uncovered, 25 minutes or until heated through. Serve with your favorite dippers.   *Makes 2½ cups dip*

SEAFOOD ARTICHOKE DIP: Add 1 can (6 ounces) crabmeat, drained and flaked.

ITALIAN ARTICHOKE DIP: Add ½ cup shredded mozzarella cheese (about 2 ounces) and ¼ cup drained and chopped sun-dried tomatoes.

ROASTED RED PEPPER ARTICHOKE DIP: Add ½ cup shredded mozzarella cheese (about 2 ounces) and ½ cup drained and chopped roasted red peppers.

MEXICAN ARTICHOKE DIP: Omit Parmesan cheese and add 1 can (4 ounces) diced green chilies, undrained, 1 cup shredded Monterey Jack cheese (about 4 ounces), ¼ cup chopped cilantro, ½ teaspoon ground cumin and hot pepper sauce to taste.

Brie Bites

Festive Taco Cups

    1 tablespoon vegetable oil

    ½ cup chopped onion

    ½ pound ground turkey or ground beef

    1 clove garlic, minced

    ½ teaspoon dried oregano

    ½ teaspoon chili powder or taco seasoning

    ¼ teaspoon salt

    1¼ cups (5 ounces) shredded taco-flavored cheese or Mexican cheese blend, divided

    1 can (11½ ounces) refrigerated corn breadstick dough

    Chopped fresh tomato and sliced green onion (optional)

1. Heat oil in large skillet over medium heat. Add onion; cook until tender. Add turkey; cook until turkey is no longer pink, stirring occasionally. Stir in garlic, oregano, chili powder and salt. Remove from heat and stir in ½ cup cheese; set aside.

2. Preheat oven to 375°F. Lightly grease 36 mini (1¾-inch) muffin pan cups. Remove dough from container but do not unroll. Separate dough into 8 pieces at perforations. Divide each piece into 3 pieces; roll or pat each into 3-inch circle. Press circles into prepared muffin cups.

3. Fill each cup with 1½ to 2 teaspoons turkey mixture. Bake 10 minutes. Sprinkle tops of taco cups with remaining ¾ cup cheese; bake 2 to 3 minutes more until cheese is melted. Garnish with tomato and green onion.   *Makes 36 taco cups*

Turkey Canapés

    8 JENNIE-O TURKEY STORE® Turkey Pastrami, turkey salami or turkey ham slices

    32 buttery round crackers, wheat crackers or rye crackers

    ¾ cup (6 ounces) cream cheese with chives or herb-flavored cream cheese

    1 small cucumber

    Fresh dill (optional)

Cut each slice of turkey into quarters. Spread each cracker with about 1 teaspoon cream cheese. Fold turkey quarters in half; place turkey on cream cheese. Cut cucumber lengthwise in half; cut each half into ¼-inch slices. Top each cracker with cucumber slice and garnish with fresh dill, if desired.   *Makes 32 servings*

Festive Taco Cups

Saucy Mini Franks

½ cup *French's®* Honey Mustard

½ cup chili sauce or ketchup

½ cup grape jelly

1 tablespoon *Frank's® RedHot®* Original Cayenne Pepper Sauce

1 pound mini cocktail franks *or* 1 pound cooked meatballs

1. Combine mustard, chili sauce, grape jelly and **Frank's RedHot** Sauce in saucepan.

2. Add cocktail franks. Simmer and stir 5 minutes or until jelly is melted and franks are hot.

Makes about 6 servings

Easy Sausage Empanadas

¼ pound bulk pork sausage

1 (15-ounce) package refrigerated pie crusts (2 crusts)

2 tablespoons finely chopped onion

⅛ teaspoon garlic powder

⅛ teaspoon ground cumin

⅛ teaspoon dried oregano

1 tablespoon chopped pimiento-stuffed green olives

1 tablespoon chopped raisins

1 egg, separated

Let pie crusts stand at room temperature for 20 minutes or according to package directions. Crumble sausage into medium skillet. Add onion, garlic powder, cumin and oregano; cook over medium-high heat until sausage is no longer pink. Drain drippings. Stir in olives and raisins. Beat egg yolk slightly; stir into sausage mixture, mixing well. Carefully unfold crusts. Cut into desired shapes using 3-inch cookie cutters. Place about 2 teaspoons sausage filling on half the cutouts. Top with remaining cutouts. (Or, use round cutter, top with sausage filling and fold dough over to create half-moon shape.) Moisten fingers with water and pinch dough to seal edges. Slightly beat egg white; gently brush over tops of empanadas. Bake in 425°F oven 15 to 18 minutes or until golden brown. *Makes 12 appetizer servings*

Favorite recipe from **National Pork Board**

Saucy Mini Franks

Chile 'n' Cheese Spirals

4 ounces cream cheese, softened

1 cup (4 ounces) shredded cheddar cheese

1 can (4 ounces) ORTEGA® Diced Green Chiles

3 green onions, sliced

½ cup chopped red bell pepper

1 can (2.25 ounces) chopped ripe olives

4 (8-inch) taco-size flour tortillas

ORTEGA Salsa (any variety)

COMBINE cream cheese, cheddar cheese, chiles, green onions, pepper and olives in medium bowl.

SPREAD ½ cup cheese mixture on each tortilla; roll up. Wrap each roll in plastic wrap; chill for 1 hour.

REMOVE plastic wrap; slice each roll into six ¾-inch pieces. Serve with salsa for dipping.

Makes 24 appetizers

TIP: Chile 'n' Cheese Spirals can be made ahead and kept in the refrigerator for 1 to 2 days.

Bacon-Wrapped Breadsticks

8 slices bacon

16 garlic-flavored breadsticks (about 8 inches long)

¾ cup grated Parmesan cheese

2 tablespoons chopped fresh parsley (optional)

1. Cut bacon slices in half lengthwise. Wrap half slice of bacon diagonally around each breadstick. Combine Parmesan cheese and parsley, if desired, in shallow dish.

2. Place 4 breadsticks on double layer of paper towels in microwave oven. Microwave on HIGH 2 to 3 minutes or until bacon is cooked through. Immediately roll breadsticks in Parmesan mixture to coat. Repeat with remaining breadsticks.

Makes 16 breadsticks

Chile 'n' Cheese Spirals

Fried Calamari with Tartar Sauce

Tartar Sauce (recipe follows)
1 pound cleaned squid (body tubes, tentacles or a combination)
1 egg
1 tablespoon milk
¾ cup plain dry bread crumbs
Vegetable oil
Lemon wedges (optional)

1. Prepare Tartar Sauce; set aside. Rinse squid under cold running water. Cut each squid body tube crosswise into ¼-inch rings. Pat pieces thoroughly dry with paper towels.

2. Beat egg and milk in small bowl. Add squid pieces; stir to coat. Spread bread crumbs on plate. Dip squid in bread crumbs; place in shallow bowl or on waxed paper. Let stand 10 to 15 minutes before frying.

3. To deep fry squid,* heat 1½ inches oil in large saucepan to 350°F. (Caution: Squid will pop and spatter during frying; do not stand too close to pan.) Adjust heat to maintain temperature. Fry 8 to 10 pieces of squid at a time in hot oil 45 seconds or until light brown. Remove with slotted spoon; drain on paper towels. Repeat with remaining squid. *Do not overcook squid or it will become tough.*

4. Serve hot with Tartar Sauce and lemon wedges, if desired.   *Makes 3 to 4 servings*

*To shallow fry squid, heat about ¼ inch oil in large skillet over medium-high heat; reduce heat to medium. Add single layer of squid to hot oil without crowding. Cook, turning once, 1 minute per side or until light brown. Drain on paper towels. Repeat with remaining squid.

Tartar Sauce

1⅓ cups mayonnaise
1 green onion, thinly sliced
2 tablespoons chopped fresh parsley
1 tablespoon drained capers, minced
1 small sweet gherkin or pickle, minced

Combine mayonnaise, green onion, parsley, capers and gherkin in small bowl; mix well. Cover and refrigerate until ready to serve.   *Makes about 1½ cups*

Fried Calamari with Tartar Sauce

Rice & Artichoke Phyllo Triangles

1 box UNCLE BEN'S® Butter & Herb Fast Cook Recipe Long Grain & Wild Rice

1 jar (6½ ounces) marinated quartered artichokes, drained and finely chopped

2 tablespoons grated Parmesan cheese

1 tablespoon minced onion or 1 green onion with top, finely chopped

⅓ cup plain yogurt or sour cream

10 sheets frozen phyllo dough, thawed

1. Prepare rice according to package directions. Cool completely.

2. Preheat oven to 375°F. In medium bowl, combine rice, artichokes, Parmesan cheese and onion; mix well. Stir in yogurt until well blended.

3. Place one sheet of phyllo dough on damp kitchen towel. (Keep remaining dough covered.) Lightly spray dough with nonstick cooking spray. Fold dough in half by bringing short sides of dough together; spray lightly with additional cooking spray.

4. Cut dough into four equal strips, each about 3¼ inches wide. For each appetizer, spoon about 1 tablespoon rice mixture onto dough about 1 inch from end of each strip. Fold 1 corner over filling to make triangle. Continue folding as you would fold a flag to form a triangle that encloses filling. Repeat with remaining dough and filling.

5. Place triangles on greased baking sheets. Spray triangles with nonstick cooking spray. Bake 12 to 15 minutes or until golden brown. *Makes 40 appetizers*

Tips: To simplify preparation, the rice mixture can be prepared a day ahead, covered and refrigerated until ready to use. Use a pizza cutter to cut phyllo dough into strips.

Rice & Artichoke Phyllo Triangles

Louisiana Hot and Spicy Shrimp

1½ pounds uncooked medium shrimp, peeled and deveined
1 cup LAWRY'S® Louisiana Red Pepper Marinade With Lemon Juice, divided
Wooden skewers, soaked in water for 15 minutes

In large resealable plastic bag, combine shrimp and ¾ cup Louisiana Red Pepper Marinade; turn to coat. Seal bag and marinate in refrigerator for 30 minutes. Remove shrimp from Marinade; discard Marinade.

On wooden skewers, thread shrimp. Grill, brushing with remaining ¼ cup Marinade, until shrimp turn pink.   *Makes 6 servings*

Prep Time: 10 minutes
Marinate Time: 30 minutes
Cook Time: 6 minutes

Cheesy Sausage Tidbits

1 (12-ounce) package BOB EVANS® Original Links
2 cups (8 ounces) shredded sharp Cheddar cheese
1¼ cups all-purpose flour
½ cup butter or margarine, melted
½ teaspoon paprika
⅛ teaspoon salt

Cook sausage in medium skillet until browned; drain on paper towels. Cut each link into 4 equal pieces. Preheat oven to 400°F. To prepare dough, combine cheese, flour, butter, paprika and salt; mix well. Wrap rounded teaspoon of dough around each piece of sausage, rolling dough in palms to form a ball. Place on ungreased baking sheet. Bake 15 to 20 minutes or until slightly browned. Serve hot. Refrigerate leftovers.   *Makes 56 tidbits*

NOTE: Cheesy Sausage Tidbits may be prepared ahead, covered and refrigerated overnight or frozen up to 1 month before baking. If frozen, they may be baked unthawed.

Louisiana Hot and Spicy Shrimp

Soups & SALADS

Sweet Potato Bisque (page 48)

Salmon Salad with Basil Vinaigrette (page 58)

Double Corn Chowder with Sausage (page 38)

Mango-Shrimp Salad

6 tablespoons picante sauce or salsa

2 tablespoons mango or peach chutney

2 tablespoons Dijon mustard

2 tablespoons lime juice

8 cups torn Boston or red leaf lettuce

12 ounces medium or large cooked shrimp, peeled and deveined

1 cup diced ripe avocado

1 cup diced ripe mango or papaya

⅔ cup red or yellow bell pepper strips

3 tablespoons chopped cilantro (optional)

Combine picante sauce, chutney, mustard and lime juice in small bowl; mix well. Combine lettuce, shrimp, avocado, mango, bell pepper and cilantro, if desired, in medium bowl. Add chutney mixture; toss well and transfer to serving plates.   *Makes 4 servings*

Double Corn Chowder with Sausage

1 package JENNIE-O TURKEY STORE® Lean Turkey Bratwurst

1 cup chopped onion

2 cups half-and-half or whole milk

1 can (15 ounces) cream-style corn

1 cup fresh or frozen corn kernels

½ cup finely diced red or green bell pepper

¼ teaspoon freshly ground black pepper

¼ teaspoon hot pepper sauce

½ cup seasoned croutons

Chopped chives or green onion tops (optional)

Crumble bratwurst into large saucepan; discard casings. Add onion; cook over medium heat 8 minutes, breaking up bratwurst into chunks. Add half-and-half, cream-style corn, corn kernels, bell pepper, black pepper and hot pepper sauce. Simmer uncovered 15 minutes, stirring occasionally. Ladle into soup bowls; top with croutons and chives, if desired.

Makes 6 servings

Mango-Shrimp Salad

Easy Tomato Minestrone

    3 slices bacon, diced
    ½ cup chopped onion
    1 large clove garlic, minced
  3½ cups water
    2 cans (10½ ounces each) condensed beef broth, undiluted
    1 can (15 ounces) Great Northern beans, undrained
    1 can (6 ounces) CONTADINA® Tomato Paste
    ¼ cup chopped fresh parsley
    1 teaspoon dried oregano leaves, crushed
    1 teaspoon dried basil leaves, crushed
    ¼ teaspoon pepper
    ½ cup dry pasta shells, macaroni or vermicelli, broken into 1-inch pieces
    1 package (16 ounces) frozen mixed Italian vegetables
    ½ cup grated Parmesan cheese (optional)

1. Sauté bacon, onion and garlic in large saucepan until onion is translucent.

2. Stir in water, broth, beans and liquid, tomato paste, parsley, oregano, basil, pepper and pasta; heat to boiling.

3. Reduce heat; simmer 15 minutes. Mix in vegetables; cook additional 10 minutes. Serve with Parmesan cheese, if desired.   *Makes about 8 servings*

Easy Tomato Minestrone

Mediterranean Shrimp and Feta Spring Salad

1 pound large raw shrimp, unpeeled

1 teaspoon salt

4 cups (6 ounces) baby spinach

2 large plum tomatoes, cored and chopped

2 ounces feta cheese, crumbled

¼ cup chopped green onions

¼ cup coarsely chopped pitted kalamata olives

1 tablespoon minced fresh oregano or basil

3 tablespoons extra-virgin olive oil

1 tablespoon red wine vinegar

1 tablespoon small capers

½ teaspoon freshly ground black pepper

1. Place shrimp in large saucepan with 1 quart water. Add salt; bring to simmer over medium-high heat. Simmer 8 to 10 minutes or until shrimp are firm and white. Drain and set aside until cool enough to handle.

2. Peel shrimp; place in large serving bowl. Add spinach, tomatoes, feta, green onions, olives and oregano.

3. Combine olive oil, vinegar, capers and pepper in small bowl; mix well. Pour over salad and toss gently. *Makes 4 servings*

NOTE: Kalamata olives are almond-shaped with a dark purplish-black color. They are soaked in a wine vinegar marinade and have a rich, fruity flavor. These olives are sold both pitted and unpitted.

Mediterranean Shrimp and Feta Spring Salad

Cream of Asparagus Soup

　1 pound fresh asparagus

3½ cups chicken broth, divided

　¼ cup (½ stick) butter

　¼ cup all-purpose flour

　½ cup light cream

　½ teaspoon salt

　⅛ teaspoon black pepper

1. Trim off and discard tough ends of asparagus. Cut asparagus into 1-inch pieces. Combine asparagus and 1 cup broth in medium saucepan; cook 10 to 12 minutes or until tender.

2. Remove 1 cup asparagus pieces; set aside. Purée remaining asparagus pieces with broth in blender or food processor.

3. Melt butter in large saucepan. Stir in flour. Gradually add remaining 2½ cups broth; cook, stirring occasionally, until slightly thickened. Stir in cream, salt, pepper, puréed asparagus mixture and asparagus pieces; heat through.　　　　　*Makes 6 to 8 servings*

Classic Coleslaw

　1 cup **HELLMANN'S® or BEST FOODS® Real Mayonnaise**

　3 tablespoons lemon juice

　2 tablespoons sugar

　1 teaspoon salt

　6 cups shredded cabbage

　1 cup shredded carrots

　½ cup chopped green bell pepper

In large bowl, combine Hellmann's or Best Foods Real Mayonnaise, lemon juice, sugar and salt. Stir in cabbage, carrots and green pepper. Chill, if desired.　　　　*Makes 6 cups*

TIP: Also terrific with Hellmann's® or Best Foods® Canola Real Mayonnaise.

Cream of Asparagus Soup

Thai Peanut Salad

- **1 cup picante sauce**
- **¼ cup chunky-style peanut butter**
- **2 tablespoons honey**
- **2 tablespoons orange juice**
- **1 teaspoon soy sauce**
- **½ teaspoon ground ginger**
- **2 cups (12 ounces) chopped HORMEL® CURE 81® ham**
- **1 (7-ounce) package spaghetti, cooked and drained**
- **¼ cup dry roasted unsalted peanuts**
- **¼ cup red bell pepper, cut into julienne strips**
- **2 tablespoons chopped cilantro**

In small saucepan, combine picante sauce, peanut butter, honey, orange juice, soy sauce and ginger. Cook and stir over low heat until mixture is smooth. Add ¼ cup sauce mixture to ham. Gently toss remaining sauce mixture with hot cooked pasta. Toss pasta mixture with ham mixture, peanuts and pepper strips. Cover and chill 1 to 2 hours. Before serving, sprinkle with cilantro.　　　　　　　　　　　　　　　*Makes 4 servings*

Mediterranean Mozzarella Salad

- **1 pound fresh bocconcini (mozzarella cheese balls) or mozzarella, cut into chunks**
- **2 large tomatoes, cut into chunks**
- **1 jar (7½ ounces) roasted red peppers, drained and coarsely chopped**
- **½ cup WISH-BONE® Balsamic Vinaigrette Dressing**
- **¼ cup loosely packed fresh basil leaves, chopped (optional)**

In large bowl, combine all ingredients. Season, if desired, with salt and ground black pepper. Cover and refrigerate at least 30 minutes. Stir well before serving.　　*Makes 6 servings*

Prep Time: 15 minutes
Chill Time: 30 minutes

Thai Peanut Salad

Sweet Potato Bisque

1 pound sweet potatoes, peeled and cut into 2-inch chunks

2 teaspoons butter

½ cup minced onion

1 teaspoon curry powder

½ teaspoon ground coriander

¼ teaspoon salt

⅔ cup unsweetened apple juice

1 cup buttermilk

¼ cup water

Fresh snipped chives (optional)

1. Place potatoes in large saucepan; cover with water. Bring to a boil over high heat. Cook, uncovered, 15 minutes or until potatoes are fork-tender. Drain and run under cold water until cool enough to handle.

2. Meanwhile, melt butter in small saucepan over medium heat. Add onion; cook and stir 2 minutes. Stir in curry powder, coriander and salt; cook and stir about 45 seconds. Remove saucepan from heat; stir in apple juice. Set aside until potatoes have cooled.

3. Combine potatoes, buttermilk and onion mixture in food processor or blender; cover and process until smooth. Pour mixture back into large saucepan; stir in ¼ cup water, as needed, to thin to desired consistency. (If soup is still too thick, add additional 1 to 2 tablespoons water.) Cook and stir over medium heat until heated through. Do not boil. Garnish with chives.   *Makes 4 servings*

Sweet Potato Bisque

Market Salad

3 eggs

4 cups washed mixed baby salad greens

2 cups green beans, cut into 1½-inch pieces, cooked and drained

4 thick slices bacon, crisp-cooked and crumbled

1 tablespoon minced fresh basil, chives or Italian parsley

3 tablespoons olive oil

1 tablespoon red wine vinegar

1 teaspoon Dijon mustard

¼ teaspoon salt

¼ teaspoon black pepper

1. Place eggs in small saucepan with water to cover; bring to a boil over medium-high heat. Immediately remove from heat. Cover; let stand 10 minutes. Drain; cool eggs to room temperature.

2. Combine salad greens, green beans, bacon and basil in large serving bowl. Peel and coarsely chop eggs; add to serving bowl. Combine oil, vinegar, mustard, salt and pepper in small bowl; drizzle over salad. Toss gently to coat.   *Makes 4 servings*

Classic Mandarin Orange Salad

½ pound spinach or mixed greens

1 can (11 or 15 ounces) DOLE® Mandarin Oranges, drained

½ cup sliced ripe olives

½ cup sliced red onion

½ cup balsamic vinaigrette

¼ cup crumbled feta cheese

• Combine spinach, mandarin oranges, olives and onion in large serving bowl.

• Pour vinaigrette over salad; toss to evenly coat. Top with feta cheese.

Makes 4 servings

Prep Time: 10 minutes

Market Salad

Chicken Tortellini Soup

6 cups reduced-sodium chicken broth *or* 1 can (48 ounces) chicken broth

1 package (9 ounces) refrigerated cheese and spinach tortellini or three-cheese tortellini

1 package (about 6 ounces) refrigerated fully cooked chicken breast strips, cut into bite-size pieces

2 cups coarsely chopped baby spinach leaves

4 to 6 tablespoons grated Parmesan cheese

1 tablespoon chopped chives *or* 2 tablespoons sliced green onions

1. Bring chicken broth to a boil in large saucepan over high heat. Add tortellini. Reduce heat to medium; cook 5 minutes. Stir in chicken and spinach.

2. Reduce heat to low. Cook 3 minutes or until chicken is hot. Sprinkle with Parmesan cheese and chives.   *Makes 4 servings*

Warm Mediterranean Rice Salad

1½ cups uncooked UNCLE BEN'S® ORIGINAL CONVERTED® Brand Rice

2 teaspoons dried basil

½ cup red wine vinaigrette, divided

1 can (6 ounces) solid white tuna in water, drained and flaked

1 cup chopped green bell pepper

1 cup chopped tomato

½ cup diced red onion

½ cup (about 18 to 20) Kalamata or pitted black olives

1. Prepare rice according to package directions. Stir basil and about ⅓ cup vinaigrette into rice.

2. Meanwhile, combine tuna, bell pepper, tomato and red onion in large salad bowl.

3. Add rice mixture to tuna and vegetables in salad bowl. Stir in remaining vinaigrette and olives.   *Makes 6 servings*

Chicken Tortellini Soup

Santa Fe BBQ Ranch Salad

    1 cup *Cattlemen's*® Golden Honey Barbecue Sauce, divided
    ½ cup ranch salad dressing
    1 pound boneless, skinless chicken
  12 cups washed and torn Romaine lettuce
    1 small red onion, thinly sliced
    1 small ripe avocado, diced
    4 ripe plum tomatoes, sliced
    2 cups shredded Monterey Jack cheese
    ½ cup cooked, crumbled bacon

1. Prepare BBQ Ranch Dressing: Combine ½ cup barbecue sauce and salad dressing in small bowl; reserve.

2. Grill or broil chicken over medium-high heat 10 minutes until no longer pink in center. Cut into strips and toss with remaining ½ cup barbecue sauce.

3. Toss lettuce, onion, avocado, tomatoes, cheese and bacon in large bowl. Transfer to salad plates, dividing evenly. Top with chicken and serve with BBQ Ranch Dressing.

Makes 4 servings

Prep Time: 15 minutes
Cook Time: 10 minutes

Tip: Serve **Cattlemen's**® Golden Honey Barbecue Sauce as a dipping sauce with chicken nuggets or seafood kabobs.

Santa Fe BBQ Ranch Salad

Black & White Mexican Bean Soup

- 1 tablespoon vegetable oil
- 1 cup chopped onion
- 1 clove garlic, minced
- ¼ cup flour
- 1 package (1.25 ounces) ORTEGA® Taco Seasoning Mix
- 2 cups milk
- 1 can (14 ounces) chicken broth
- 1 package (16 ounces) frozen corn
- 1 can (15½ ounces) great northern beans, drained
- 1 can (15½ ounces) black beans, drained
- 1 can (4 ounces) ORTEGA Diced Green Chiles
- 2 tablespoons chopped cilantro

HEAT oil in large pan or Dutch oven over medium-high heat. Add onion and garlic; cook until onion is tender.

STIR in flour and taco seasoning mix; gradually stir in milk until blended. Add remaining ingredients except cilantro.

BRING to a boil, stirring constantly. Reduce heat to low; simmer for 15 minutes or until thickened, stirring occasionally.

STIR in cilantro.   *Makes 6 servings (1⅓ cups each)*

Black & White Mexican Bean Soup

Salmon Salad with Basil Vinaigrette

Basil Vinaigrette (recipe follows)
1 **pound asparagus, trimmed**
1¼ **teaspoons salt, divided**
1 **pound salmon fillets**
1½ **teaspoons olive oil**
¼ **teaspoon black pepper**
4 **lemon wedges**

1. Prepare Basil Vinaigrette. Preheat oven to 400°F or prepare grill for direct cooking. Place 3 inches of water and 1 teaspoon salt in large saucepan or Dutch oven. Bring to a boil over high heat. Add asparagus; simmer 6 to 8 minutes or until crisp-tender. Drain and set aside.

2. Brush salmon with olive oil. Sprinkle with remaining ¼ teaspoon salt and pepper. Place fish in shallow baking pan; cook 11 to 13 minutes or fish begins to flake when tested with a fork. (Or, grill on well-oiled grid over medium-hot coals 4 or 5 minutes per side or until fish begins to flake when tested with a fork.)

3. Remove skin from salmon. Break salmon into bite-size pieces. Arrange salmon over asparagus spears on serving plate. Spoon Basil Vinaigrette over salmon. Serve with lemon wedges.   *Makes 4 servings*

Basil Vinaigrette

3 **tablespoons extra-virgin olive oil**
1 **tablespoon white wine vinegar**
1 **tablespoon minced fresh basil**
1 **clove garlic, minced**
1 **teaspoon minced fresh chives**
¼ **teaspoon black pepper**
⅛ **teaspoon salt**

Combine all ingredients in small bowl; stir until blended.   *Makes ¼ cup*

Salmon Salad with Basil Vinaigrette

Sausage & Rice Soup

- **2 tablespoons butter or margarine**
- **1 large or 2 medium leeks, white and light green parts sliced**
- **2 carrots, thinly sliced**
- **1 package (16 ounces) JENNIE-O TURKEY STORE® Extra Lean Smoked Sausage**
- **2 cups diced mixed bell peppers, preferably red and yellow**
- **2 cans (13¾ ounces each) reduced-sodium chicken broth**
- **1 cup water**
- **¾ cup quick-cooking brown rice, uncooked**
- **½ teaspoon dried sage**
- **¼ teaspoon freshly ground black pepper**
- **Chopped fresh chives (optional)**

Melt butter in large saucepan over medium heat. Add leeks and carrots; cook 5 minutes, stirring occasionally. Meanwhile, cut sausage into ½-inch slices. Add sausage to saucepan; cook 5 minutes, stirring occasionally. Add bell peppers, broth, water, rice, sage and pepper; bring to a boil over high heat. Reduce heat; simmer uncovered 15 minutes or until rice is tender. Ladle into bowls; top with chives, if desired.   *Makes 6 servings*

Romaine & Green Apple Salad with Pecans

- **6 cups torn romaine lettuce (about 7 ounces)**
- **1 large green apple, cored and thinly sliced**
- **⅓ cup WISH-BONE® Red Wine Vinaigrette Dressing**
- **⅓ cup chopped pecans, toasted**
- **½ cup crumbled blue cheese (2 ounces)**

1. In large serving bowl, toss lettuce, apple and Wish-Bone Red Wine Vinaigrette Dressing.

2. Sprinkle with pecans and cheese.   *Makes 4 servings*

TIP: Also terrific with Wish-Bone® Fat Free! Red Wine Vinaigrette Dressing.

Prep Time: 15 minutes

Sausage & Rice Soup

Crunchy Mexican Side Salad

    3 cups romaine and iceberg lettuce blend
    ½ cup grape tomatoes, halved
    ½ cup peeled and diced jicama
    ¼ cup sliced olives
    ¼ cup ORTEGA® Sliced Jalapeños, quartered
    2 tablespoons ORTEGA Taco Sauce
    1 tablespoon vegetable oil
    ⅛ teaspoon salt
       Crushed ORTEGA Taco Shells (optional)

TOSS together lettuce, tomatoes, jicama, olives and jalapeños in large bowl.

COMBINE taco sauce, oil and salt in small bowl. Stir with a fork until blended.

POUR dressing over salad; toss gently to coat. Top with taco shells, if desired.

Makes 4 servings (1 cup each)

Tip: ORTEGA® Sliced Jalapeños are available in a 12-ounce jar. They are pickled, adding great flavor and crunch to this salad.

Crunchy Mexican Side Salad

Memorable MAIN DISHES

Lickety-Split Paella Pronto (page 84) *Chicken Cassoulet (page 74)*

Turkey with Sausage & Corn Bread Stuffing (page 66)

Cajun Grilled Chicken

4 boneless skinless chicken breast halves

2 tablespoons lemon juice

3 tablespoons MRS. DASH® Extra Spicy Seasoning Blend

2 tablespoons paprika

1 tablespoon brown sugar

Cooking spray

Preheat grill to medium-high. With sharp knife, slash each piece of chicken in 2 or 3 places with ¼-inch-deep cuts. In medium bowl, combine chicken and lemon juice, turning chicken until thoroughly coated. Set aside. In separate bowl, mix Mrs. Dash® Extra Spicy Seasoning, paprika and brown sugar. Roll each piece of chicken in spice mixture until well coated. Spray grill with cooking spray and place seasoned chicken breasts on grill. Cook 5 minutes and turn. Cook 5 minutes more or until juices run clear when skewer is inserted into thickest part of chicken breast. Serve immediately.   *Makes 4 servings*

Turkey with Sausage & Corn Bread Stuffing

1 pound bulk pork sausage

1½ cups chopped onions

1 cup chopped celery

1 clove garlic, minced

1 bag (16 ounces) corn bread stuffing mix

1 can (about 14 ounces) chicken broth

2 teaspoons poultry seasoning

1 (14- to 16-pound) turkey, thawed

2 tablespoons butter, melted

Salt and black pepper

Continued on page 68

Cajun Grilled Chicken

Turkey with Sausage & Corn Bread Stuffing, continued

1. Preheat oven to 325°F. Cook and stir sausage in large skillet over medium heat until browned; drain. Add onions, celery and garlic to skillet; cook and stir about 5 minutes or until vegetables are tender. Stir in stuffing mix, broth and poultry seasoning until blended.

2. Spoon stuffing into turkey cavity; close with metal skewers. Place turkey, breast side up, on rack in shallow roasting pan. Brush butter over outside of turkey; season with salt and pepper. Insert ovenproof meat thermometer into thickest part of thigh not touching bone.

3. Bake turkey uncovered 4 to 5 hours, basting occasionally with pan drippings, until temperature reaches 180°F. Let stand 20 minutes before carving.   *Makes 10 servings*

NOTE: If turkey is browning too quickly, tent loosely with foil, being careful not to touch meat thermometer.

Cranberry-Glazed Ham

    1 (5- to 6-pound) fully cooked spiral sliced ham half*
    ¾ cup cranberry sauce or cranberry chutney
    ¼ cup Dijon or hot Dijon mustard
    1 teaspoon ground cinnamon
    ¼ teaspoon ground allspice

A whole ham is usually 10 to 12 pounds and serves 24. Double glaze ingredients if using a whole ham.

1. Preheat oven to 300°F. Place ham in large roasting pan lined with heavy-duty aluminum foil. Combine cranberry sauce, mustard, cinnamon and allspice; mix well. Spread half of mixture evenly over top of ham (glaze will melt and spread as it cooks).

2. Bake 1 hour; spread remaining cranberry mixture over top of ham. Continue to bake until internal temperature of ham reaches 140°F, about 1 hour. Transfer ham to carving board; let stand 5 minutes before serving.   *Makes 10 to 12 servings*

Cranberry-Glazed Ham

Gemelli & Grilled Summer Vegetables

    2 large bell peppers (red and yellow)
   12 stalks asparagus
    2 slices red onion
    3 tablespoons plus 1 teaspoon extra-virgin olive oil, divided
    6 ounces (2¼ cups) gemelli or rotini pasta
    2 tablespoons pine nuts
    1 clove garlic
    1 cup loosely packed basil leaves
   ¼ cup grated Parmesan cheese
   ¼ teaspoon salt
   ¼ teaspoon black pepper
    1 cup grape or cherry tomatoes

1. Prepare grill for direct cooking. Cut bell peppers in half; remove and discard seeds. Place asparagus and onion on large plate; coat with 1 teaspoon olive oil.

2. Grill bell peppers, skin side down, on covered grill over medium heat 10 to 12 minutes or until skins are blackened. Place peppers in paper bag; let stand 15 minutes. Remove and discard blackened skin. Cut into chunks.

3. Cook pasta according to package directions; drain and return to pan. Meanwhile, grill asparagus and onion on covered grill over medium heat 8 to 10 minutes or until tender, turning once. Cut asparagus into 2-inch pieces; cut onion into small pieces. Add vegetables to pasta.

4. Place pine nuts and garlic in food processor; process until coarsely chopped. Add basil; process until finely chopped. While processor is running, add remaining 3 tablespoons olive oil. Stir in cheese, salt and pepper. Add basil mixture and tomatoes to pasta; toss until pasta is coated. Serve immediately. *Makes 4 servings*

Gemelli & Grilled Summer Vegetables

Roast Pork with Tart Cherries

1 boneless rolled pork roast (3½ to 4 pounds)

3 teaspoons prepared grated horseradish, divided

1 teaspoon ground coriander

½ teaspoon black pepper

1 can (16 ounces) pitted tart cherries, undrained

½ cup chicken broth

⅓ cup Madeira wine or dry sherry

4 teaspoons grated orange peel

1 tablespoon packed brown sugar

1 tablespoon Dijon mustard

⅛ teaspoon ground cloves

1. Preheat oven to 400°F. Place pork on rack in shallow roasting pan.

2. Combine 2 teaspoons horseradish, coriander and pepper in small bowl. Rub over pork. Roast pork 10 minutes; remove from oven. *Reduce oven temperature to 350°F.*

3. Add cherries with juice and broth to pan. Cover pan loosely with foil. Roast about 1 hour 30 minutes, basting every 20 minutes, or until internal temperature of roast reaches 165°F when tested with meat thermometer inserted into the thickest part of roast. (Uncover roast during last 20 minutes of cooking.)

4. Transfer pork to cutting board; cover with foil. Let stand 10 to 15 minutes before carving. (Internal temperature will continue to rise 5° to 10°F during this time.)

5. Meanwhile, remove rack from roasting pan. Strain contents of pan into small saucepan, reserving cherries. Stir wine, orange peel, sugar, mustard, remaining 1 teaspoon horseradish and cloves into saucepan. Bring to a boil over medium-high heat. Boil 10 minutes or until sauce is thickened. Stir in reserved cherries.

6. Carve pork into thin slices; place on serving platter. Pour half of cherry sauce around pork; serve with remaining sauce. *Makes 8 servings*

Roast Pork with Tart Cherries

Chicken Cassoulet

  4 slices bacon
¼ cup all-purpose flour
   Salt and black pepper
1¾ pounds bone-in chicken pieces
  2 cooked chicken sausages, cut into ¼-inch pieces
  1 onion, chopped
1½ cups diced red and green bell peppers (2 small bell peppers)
  2 cloves garlic, finely chopped
  1 teaspoon dried thyme
   Olive oil
  2 cans (about 15 ounces each) cannellini or Great Northern beans,
     rinsed and drained
½ cup dry white wine or water

1. Preheat oven to 350°F. Cook bacon in large skillet over medium-high heat until crisp. Drain on paper towels. Crumble into 1-inch pieces.

2. Pour off all but 2 tablespoons fat from skillet. Place flour in shallow bowl; season with salt and black pepper. Dip chicken pieces in flour mixture; shake off excess. Brown chicken in batches in large skillet over medium-high heat; remove and set aside. Lightly brown sausages in same skillet; remove and set aside.

3. Add onion, bell peppers, garlic, thyme, salt and black pepper to skillet; cook and stir over medium heat 5 minutes or until softened, adding olive oil as needed to prevent sticking. Transfer onion mixture to 13×9-inch baking dish. Add beans; mix well. Top with chicken, sausages and bacon. Add wine to skillet; cook and stir over medium heat, scraping up brown bits on bottom of pan. Pour over casserole.

4. Bake, covered, 40 minutes. Uncover and bake 15 minutes more or until chicken is no longer pink in center. *Makes 6 servings*

Chicken Cassoulet

Oven-Baked Stew

  2 pounds boneless beef chuck or round steak, cut into 1-inch cubes
  ¼ **cup all-purpose flour**
1⅓ **cups sliced carrots**
  1 can (14 to 16 ounces) whole peeled tomatoes, undrained and chopped
  1 envelope LIPTON® RECIPE SECRETS® Onion Soup Mix*
  ½ **cup dry red wine or water**
  1 cup fresh or canned sliced mushrooms
  1 package (8 ounces) medium or broad egg noodles, cooked and drained

Also terrific with LIPTON® RECIPE SECRETS® Beefy Onion or Onion Mushroom Soup Mix.

1. Preheat oven to 425°F. In 2½-quart shallow casserole, toss beef with flour, then bake uncovered, 20 minutes, stirring once.

2. *Reduce heat to 350°F.* Stir in carrots, tomatoes, soup mix and wine.

3. Bake covered 1½ hours or until beef is tender. Stir in mushrooms and bake covered, an additional 10 minutes. Serve over hot noodles.   *Makes 8 servings*

SLOW COOKER METHOD: In slow cooker, toss beef with flour. Add carrots, tomatoes, soup mix and wine. Cook covered, on LOW 8 to 10 hours. Add mushrooms; cook covered, on LOW 30 minutes or until beef is tender. Serve over hot noodles.

Prep Time: 20 minutes
Cook Time: 2 hours

Oven-Baked Stew

Glazed Cornish Hens

2 fresh or thawed frozen Cornish game hens (1½ pounds each)

3 tablespoons fresh lemon juice

1 clove garlic, minced

¼ cup orange marmalade

1 tablespoon coarse grain or country-style mustard

2 teaspoons grated fresh ginger

1. Remove giblets from cavities of hens; reserve for another use or discard. Split hens in half on cutting board with sharp knife or poultry shears, cutting through breastbones and backbones. Rinse hens with cold water; pat dry with paper towels. Place hen halves in large resealable food storage bag.

2. Combine lemon juice and garlic in small bowl; pour over hens in bag. Seal bag tightly, turning to coat. Marinate in refrigerator 30 minutes.

3. Meanwhile, prepare grill for direct grilling.

4. Drain hens; discard marinade. Place hens, skin sides up, on grid. Grill hens, covered, over medium-hot coals 20 minutes.

5. Meanwhile, combine marmalade, mustard and ginger in small bowl. Brush half of marmalade mixture evenly over hens. Grill, covered, 10 minutes. Brush with remaining mixture. Grill, covered, 5 to 10 minutes or until hens are cooked through and juices run clear. Serve immediately.   *Makes 4 servings*

Glazed Cornish Hens

Swordfish Pomodoro

1½ **pounds swordfish steaks (¾ inch thick)**

    Salt and black pepper

1 **tablespoon all-purpose flour**

2 **teaspoons olive oil**

1 **medium onion, halved and cut into thin slices**

1 **clove garlic, minced**

1½ **cups chopped seeded tomatoes**

⅓ **cup drained mild giardiniera***

2 **tablespoons dry white wine (optional)**

1 **tablespoon chopped fresh oregano *or* 1 teaspoon dried oregano**

2 **tablespoons canola oil**

*Giardiniera is an Italian term for pickled vegetables. Available mild or hot, you can find giardiniera in the pickle or ethnic foods section of the grocery store.

1. Season fish with salt and pepper. Dust fish with flour; set aside.

2. Heat olive oil in medium skillet over medium heat. Add onion; cook and stir 4 minutes or until tender. Add garlic; cook and stir 30 seconds. Add tomatoes; cook 3 minutes, stirring occasionally. Stir in giardiniera, wine, oregano and ¼ teaspoon salt. Cook 3 minutes or until most of liquid has evaporated.

3. Meanwhile, heat canola oil in large nonstick skillet over medium-high heat. Cook fish 7 minutes, turning once, or until fish begins to flake when tested with fork. Serve tomato mixture over fish.   *Makes 6 servings*

Prep Time: 10 minutes
Cook Time: 20 minutes

Swordfish Pomodoro

Peppered Steaks with Caramelized Onions

2 beef shoulder center steaks (Ranch steaks), cut 1 inch thick
    (about 8 ounces each)

1 pound unpeeled small red and brown-skinned potatoes, quartered

1 teaspoon olive oil

½ teaspoon dried thyme

⅛ teaspoon salt

2 teaspoons seasoned pepper blend

    Caramelized Onions and Sautéed Spinach (recipe follows)

1. Preheat oven to 425°F. Place potatoes on rimmed baking sheet. Sprinkle with oil, thyme and salt; toss to coat. Roast in oven 30 to 40 minutes or until tender, turning occasionally.

2. Meanwhile, press pepper blend onto beef steaks. Heat large nonstick skillet over medium heat until hot. Place steaks in skillet, cook 13 to 16 minutes for medium rare to medium doneness, turning twice.

3. Carve steaks; season with salt as desired. Top with onions; serve with potatoes and spinach.   *Makes 4 servings*

CARAMELIZED ONIONS AND SAUTÉED SPINACH: Heat 1 tablespoon butter in large nonstick skillet over medium heat until melted. Add 1 large yellow onion, cut ¼ inch thick; cook 18 to 21 minutes or until caramelized, stirring frequently. Remove onion from skillet; keep warm. Heat 2 teaspoons olive oil and 1 large clove minced garlic over medium heat in same skillet about 30 seconds or until fragrant. Add 8 cups spinach and ⅛ teaspoon salt. Toss to coat and cook 1 minute or until just wilted, stirring frequently. Serve immediately.

Prep and Cook Time: 45 minutes to 1 hour

*Favorite recipe from **National Cattlemen's Beef Association on behalf of The Beef Checkoff***

Peppered Steaks with Caramelized Onions

Lickety-Split Paella Pronto

1 tablespoon olive oil

1 large onion, chopped

2 cloves garlic, minced

1 jar (16 ounces) salsa

1 can (about 14 ounces) diced tomatoes

1 can (14 ounces) artichoke hearts, drained and quartered

1 can (about 14 ounces) chicken broth

1 package (about 8 ounces) uncooked yellow rice

1 can (12 ounces) solid albacore tuna, drained and flaked

1 package (about 9 ounces) frozen green peas

2 tablespoons finely chopped green onions (optional)

2 tablespoons finely chopped red bell pepper (optional)

1. Heat oil in large nonstick skillet over medium heat. Add onion and garlic; cook and stir about 5 minutes or until onion is tender.

2. Stir in salsa, tomatoes, artichokes, broth and rice; bring to a boil over high heat. Reduce heat to low; cover and simmer 15 minutes.

3. Stir in tuna and peas. Cover and cook 5 to 10 minutes or until rice is tender and tuna and peas are heated through. Garnish with green onions and red bell pepper.

Makes 4 to 6 servings

Tip: Albacore tuna has the lightest flesh of all tunas; it is the only one that can be called "white."

Lickety-Split Paella Pronto

Mediterranean Chicken Kabobs

2 pounds boneless skinless chicken breasts or chicken tenders,
  cut into 1-inch pieces

1 small eggplant, peeled and cut into 1-inch pieces

1 medium zucchini, cut crosswise into ½-inch slices

2 medium onions, each cut into 8 wedges

16 medium mushrooms, stems removed

16 cherry tomatoes

1 cup reduced-sodium chicken broth

⅔ cup balsamic vinegar

3 tablespoons olive oil

2 tablespoons dried mint

4 teaspoons dried basil

1 tablespoon dried oregano

2 teaspoons grated lemon peel

  Chopped fresh parsley (optional)

4 cups hot cooked couscous

1. Alternately thread chicken, eggplant, zucchini, onions, mushrooms and tomatoes onto 16 metal skewers; place in large baking dish.

2. Combine chicken broth, vinegar, oil, mint, basil and oregano in small bowl; pour over kabobs. Cover and marinate in refrigerator 2 hours, turning kabobs occasionally. Remove kabobs from marinade; discard marinade.

3. Preheat broiler. Broil kabobs 6 inches from heat 10 to 15 minutes or until chicken is no longer pink in center, turning kabobs halfway through cooking time.

4. Stir lemon peel and parsley into couscous; serve with kabobs.   *Makes 8 servings*

TIP: These kabobs can be grilled instead of broiled. Spray the grill grid with nonstick cooking spray, then prepare grill for direct grilling. Grill the kabobs on a covered grill over medium-hot coals 10 to 15 minutes or until the chicken is no longer pink in center. Turn the kabobs halfway through the grilling time.

Mediterranean Chicken Kabobs

Lamb Chops with Mustard Sauce

    1 teaspoon dried thyme
    ½ teaspoon salt
    ¼ teaspoon black pepper
    4 center-cut loin lamb chops (about 1½ pounds total)
    2 tablespoons canola or vegetable oil
    ¼ cup finely chopped shallots or sweet onion
    ¼ cup beef or chicken broth
    2 tablespoons Worcestershire sauce
 1½ tablespoons Dijon mustard

1. Sprinkle thyme, salt and pepper over lamb chops. Heat oil in large skillet over medium heat. Add chops; cook 4 minutes per side. Remove chops from skillet; set aside.

2. Add shallots to skillet; cook 3 minutes, stirring occasionally. Reduce heat to medium-low. Add broth, Worcestershire sauce and mustard; simmer 5 minutes or until sauce thickens slightly, stirring occasionally. Return chops to skillet; cook 2 minutes for medium-rare, turning once. Transfer to serving plates. *Makes 4 servings*

Hazelnut-Coated Salmon Steaks

    4 salmon steaks (about 5 ounces each)
    1 tablespoon apple butter
    1 tablespoon Dijon mustard
    ¼ teaspoon dried thyme
    ⅛ teaspoon black pepper
    ¼ cup chopped toasted hazelnuts

1. Preheat oven to 450°F. Place salmon in single layer in baking dish. Combine apple butter, mustard, thyme and pepper in small bowl. Brush onto salmon; top each steak with hazelnuts.

2. Bake 14 to 16 minutes or until salmon begins to flake when tested with fork. Serve with herbed rice and steamed sugar snap peas, if desired. *Makes 4 servings*

Lamb Chop with Mustard Sauce

Irish Stew in Bread

1½ **pounds lean, boned American lamb shoulder, cut into 1-inch cubes**

¼ **cup all-purpose flour**

2 **tablespoons vegetable oil**

2 **cloves garlic, crushed**

2 **cups water**

¼ **cup Burgundy wine**

5 **medium carrots, chopped**

3 **medium potatoes, peeled and sliced**

2 **large onions, peeled and chopped**

2 **ribs celery, sliced**

¾ **teaspoon black pepper**

1 **cube beef bouillon, crushed**

1 **cup frozen peas**

¼ **pound sliced fresh mushrooms**

  Round bread, unsliced*

*Stew can be served individually in small loaves or in one large loaf. Slice bread crosswise near top to form lid. Hollow larger piece, leaving 1-inch border. Fill "bowl" with hot stew; cover with "lid." Serve immediately.

Coat lamb with flour while heating oil in Dutch oven over low heat. Add lamb and garlic; cook and stir until brown. Add water, wine, carrots, potatoes, onions, celery, pepper and bouillon. Cover; simmer 30 to 35 minutes.

Add peas and mushrooms. Cover; simmer 10 minutes. Bring to a boil; adjust seasonings, if necessary. Serve in bread.   *Makes 6 to 8 servings*

Favorite recipe from ***American Lamb Council***

Irish Stew in Bread

Herb Roasted Chicken

　1 whole chicken (3 to 4 pounds)
1¼ teaspoons salt, divided
　½ teaspoon black pepper, divided
　1 lemon, cut into quarters
　4 sprigs fresh rosemary, divided
　4 sprigs fresh thyme, divided
　4 cloves garlic, peeled
　2 tablespoons olive oil

1. Preheat oven to 425°F. Place chicken breast side up in shallow roasting pan. Season cavity of chicken with ½ teaspoon salt and ¼ teaspoon pepper. Fill cavity with lemon quarters, 2 sprigs rosemary, 2 sprigs thyme and garlic cloves.

2. Chop remaining rosemary and thyme leaves; combine with olive oil, remaining ¾ teaspoon salt and ¼ teaspoon pepper in small bowl. Brush mixture over chicken.

3. Roast chicken 30 minutes. *Reduce oven temperature to 375°F;* roast 35 to 45 minutes more or until meat thermometer inserted into thickest part of thigh reaches 180°F. Let stand 10 to 15 minutes before carving.　　　　　　　　　　　*Makes 4 to 5 servings*

Very Berry Pork Chops

　4 pork chops, ¾ inch thick
　2 teaspoons vegetable oil
　¼ cup strawberry preserves
　¼ cup cider vinegar
　1 tablespoon mustard

Heat oil in large skillet over medium-high heat. Add pork chops, cook and turn until brown on both sides. Reduce heat to low. In small bowl, stir together strawberry preserves, vinegar and mustard. Pour sauce over pork chops. Cover pan. Cook pork chops for 10 minutes or until sauce has thickened. To serve, spoon sauce over each chop.　　　　　　*Makes 4 servings*

Favorite recipe from **National Pork Board**

Herb Roasted Chicken

Spicy Peanut-Coconut Shrimp

¼ **cup shredded coconut**

2 **teaspoons dark sesame oil**

1 **pound large raw shrimp (thawed if frozen), peeled, deveined and patted dry**

¼ **to** ½ **teaspoon crushed red pepper flakes**

2 **tablespoons chopped fresh mint or cilantro**

¼ **cup chopped lightly salted roasted peanuts**

Fresh lime wedges

1. Toast coconut in small nonstick skillet over medium-high heat 2 to 3 minutes or until golden, stirring constantly. Immediately remove from skillet.

2. Heat oil in large nonstick skillet over medium-high heat. Add shrimp and pepper flakes; stir-fry 3 to 4 minutes until shrimp are pink and opaque. Stir in mint. Transfer to serving plates; top with toasted coconut and peanuts. Garnish with lime wedges.

Makes 4 servings

Mediterranean Grilled Steak

½ **cup WISH-BONE® Italian or Robusto Italian Dressing**

2 **large cloves garlic, finely chopped**

2 **teaspoons finely chopped fresh rosemary leaves or** ½ **teaspoon dried rosemary leaves, crushed***

1½ **pound top sirloin steak, 1-inch thick**

1. For marinade, combine Wish-Bone Italian Dressing, garlic and rosemary. In large, shallow nonaluminum baking dish or plastic bag, pour ¼ cup marinade over steak; turn to coat. Cover or close bag and marinate in refrigerator 30 minutes. Refrigerate remaining marinade.

2. Remove steak from marinade, discarding marinade. Grill steak, turning occasionally and brushing frequently with refrigerated marinade, until desired doneness.

Makes 6 servings

VARIATION: Use 1 tablespoon finely chopped fresh basil leaves or 1 teaspoon dried basil leaves, crushed, instead of rosemary.

Spicy Peanut-Coconut Shrimp

Sensational
SIDES

Carrie's Sweet Potato Casserole
(page 114)

Wild Rice, Cranberry and Apple Stuffing
(page 122)

Fiesta-Style Roasted Vegetables (page 98)

Original Ranch® Roasted Potatoes

2 pounds small red potatoes, quartered

¼ cup vegetable oil

1 packet (1 ounce) HIDDEN VALLEY® The Original Ranch® Salad Dressing & Seasoning Mix

Place potatoes in a gallon-size Glad® Zipper Storage Bag. Pour oil over potatoes. Seal bag and toss to coat. Add salad dressing & seasoning mix; seal bag and toss again until coated. Bake in an ungreased baking pan at 450°F for 30 to 35 minutes or until potatoes are brown and crisp.   *Makes 4 to 6 servings*

Fiesta-Style Roasted Vegetables

1 can (4 ounces) ORTEGA® Diced Green Chiles

3 tablespoons vinegar

2 tablespoons vegetable oil

1 package (1.25 ounces) ORTEGA Taco Seasoning Mix

1 small red bell pepper, cut into strips

1 medium zucchini, cut into ½-inch slices

1 small sweet potato, peeled, cut into ⅛-inch slices and halved

1 small red onion, cut into wedges

Nonstick cooking spray

COMBINE chiles, vinegar, oil and seasoning mix in large bowl; mix well. Add red pepper, zucchini, sweet potato and onion; toss gently to coat. Let stand at room temperature 15 minutes to marinate.

PREHEAT oven to 450°F. Cover 15×10-inch baking pan with foil and spray with cooking spray.

REMOVE vegetables from marinade with spoon, placing on prepared pan.

BAKE 20 to 25 minutes until tender and browned, stirring once.

Makes 4 servings (1 cup each)

VARIATION: Substitute yellow squash for the zucchini, if preferred.

Original Ranch® Roasted Potatoes

Savory Beets

2 tablespoons chopped onion

1 tablespoon butter or margarine

3 tablespoons honey

2 tablespoons red or white wine vinegar

Salt to taste

⅛ teaspoon ground cloves

1 can (16 ounces) sliced beets, drained

Sauté onion in butter in large skillet over medium heat until softened. Add honey, vinegar, salt and cloves; cook and stir until mixture begins to boil. Add beets; cook until thoroughly heated.

Makes 4 servings

*Favorite recipe from **National Honey Board***

Three Pepper Pilaf

1 medium yellow onion, chopped

1 cup chopped assorted bell peppers, such as yellow, green and red

2 tablespoons butter or margarine

1½ cups water

¾ cup uncooked long-grain white rice

2 teaspoons HERB-OX® chicken flavored bouillon

¼ teaspoon white pepper

3 slices HORMEL® BLACK LABEL® fully cooked bacon, crumbled or ⅓ cup HORMEL® bacon bits or pieces

In large saucepan, cook onion and peppers in hot butter until tender but not brown. Add water, uncooked rice, bouillon and white pepper. Bring to a boil. Cover, reduce heat and simmer 15 to 20 minutes or until rice is tender and liquid is absorbed. Stir in crumbled bacon.

Makes 6 servings

Prep Time: 10 minutes
Total Time: 35 minutes

Savory Beets

Ham and Potato Pancakes

¾ **pound Yukon gold potatoes, peeled, grated and squeezed dry (about 2 cups)**

¼ **cup finely chopped green onions**

2 **eggs, beaten**

1 **cup (4 to 5 ounces) finely chopped cooked ham**

¼ **cup all-purpose flour**

¼ **teaspoon salt**

¼ **teaspoon black pepper**

2 **to 3 tablespoons vegetable oil**

Chili sauce or mild fruit chutney (optional)

1. Combine grated potatoes, green onions and eggs in large bowl; mix well. Add ham, flour, salt and pepper; mix well.

2. Heat 2 tablespoons oil in large heavy skillet. Drop batter by heaping tablespoonfuls and press with back of spoon to flatten. Cook over medium-high heat 2 to 3 minutes per side. Remove to paper towels to drain. Add remaining 1 tablespoon oil, if necessary, to cook remaining batter. Serve with chili sauce, if desired.   *Makes 4 servings*

Roasted Butternut Squash

1 **pound butternut squash, peeled and cut into 1-inch cubes (about 4 cups)**

2 **medium onions, coarsely chopped**

8 **ounces carrots, peeled and cut into ½-inch diagonal slices (about 2 cups)**

Nonstick cooking spray

1 **tablespoon dark brown sugar**

¼ **teaspoon salt**

Black pepper (optional)

1 **tablespoon butter or margarine, melted**

1. Preheat oven to 400°F. Line large baking sheet with foil; coat with cooking spray. Arrange vegetables in single layer on foil; coat lightly with cooking spray. Sprinkle with brown sugar, salt and pepper, if desired.

2. Bake 30 minutes. Stir gently; bake 10 to 15 minutes more or until vegetables are tender. Remove from oven. Drizzle with butter; toss to coat.   *Makes 5 servings*

Ham and Potato Pancakes

Baked Spinach Risotto

    1 tablespoon olive oil
    1 green bell pepper, chopped
    1 medium onion, chopped
    2 cloves garlic, minced
    1 cup arborio rice
    3 cups chopped fresh spinach leaves
    1 (14½-ounce) can chicken broth
    ½ cup grated Parmesan cheese, divided
    1 tablespoon TABASCO® brand Green Pepper Sauce
    1 teaspoon salt

Preheat oven to 400°F. Grease 1½-quart casserole. Heat oil in 10-inch skillet over medium heat. Add green bell pepper, onion and garlic; cook 5 minutes. Add rice; stir to coat well. Stir in spinach, chicken broth, ¼ cup Parmesan cheese, TABASCO® Green Pepper Sauce and salt. Spoon mixture into prepared baking dish. Sprinkle with remaining ¼ cup Parmesan cheese. Bake 35 to 40 minutes or until rice is tender.   *Makes 4 servings*

Maple-Glazed Carrots & Shallots

    1 package (16 ounces) baby carrots
    1 tablespoon butter
    ½ cup thinly sliced shallots
    2 tablespoons maple syrup
    ¼ teaspoon salt
    ⅛ teaspoon white pepper

1. Place carrots in medium saucepan; add enough water to cover. Bring to a boil over high heat. Reduce heat; simmer 8 to 10 minutes or until carrots are tender. Drain and set aside.

2. In same saucepan, melt butter over medium-high heat. Add shallots; cook and stir 3 to 4 minutes or until shallots are tender and begin to brown. Add carrots, syrup, salt and pepper; cook and stir 1 to 2 minutes or until carrots are coated and heated through.

Makes 4 servings

Baked Spinach Risotto

Roast Herbed Sweet Potatoes with Bacon & Onions

3 thick slices applewood-smoked or peppered bacon, diced

2 pounds sweet potatoes, peeled and cut into 2-inch chunks

2 medium onions, cut into 8 wedges

1 teaspoon salt

1 teaspoon dried thyme

¼ teaspoon black pepper

1. Preheat oven to 375°F. Cook bacon in large heavy skillet until crisp. Remove from heat. Transfer bacon to paper towels; set aside. Add potatoes and onions to drippings in skillet; toss until coated. Stir in salt, thyme and pepper.

2. Spread mixture in single layer in ungreased 15×10-inch jelly-roll pan or shallow roasting pan. Bake 40 to 50 minutes or until golden brown and tender. Transfer to serving bowl; sprinkle with bacon. *Makes 6 to 8 servings*

Sausage & Apricot Balsamic Rice

1 (12-ounce) package sage-flavored pork sausage

⅓ cup maple syrup

6 tablespoons balsamic vinegar

3 cups cooked long grain rice

1 cup coarsely chopped roasted, salted cashew nuts

¾ cup chopped dried apricots

¼ teaspoon salt

¼ teaspoon ground black pepper

Crumble sausage into large nonstick skillet. Stirring occasionally, cook over medium heat until browned, about 10 to 15 minutes. Drain grease from pan. Add maple syrup and vinegar; cook and stir 2 to 3 minutes to blend. Add rice, cashews, apricots, salt and pepper; stir over medium heat until blended. Serve warm. *Makes 8 servings*

*Favorite recipe from **USA Rice***

Roast Herbed Sweet Potatoes with Bacon & Onions

Corn Pudding

- 1 tablespoon butter
- 1 small onion, chopped
- 1 tablespoon all-purpose flour
- 2 cups half-and-half
- 1 cup milk
- ¼ cup quick-cooking grits or polenta
- ¾ teaspoon salt
- ¼ teaspoon black pepper
- ¼ teaspoon hot pepper sauce
- 2 cups fresh or frozen corn kernels, thawed
- 1 can (4 ounces) diced mild chiles, drained
- 4 eggs, beaten

1. Preheat oven to 325°F. Grease 11×7-inch baking dish. Melt butter in large saucepan over medium heat. Add onion; cook and stir 5 minutes or until tender and light golden. Stir in flour; cook to a paste. Stir in half-and-half and milk; bring to a boil. Whisk in grits. Reduce heat to medium-low; cook, stirring frequently, 10 minutes or until thickened.

2. Remove from heat; stir in salt, pepper and hot sauce. Add corn and chiles. Stir in eggs until well blended. Pour into prepared baking dish. Bake 1 hour or until knife inserted in center of pudding comes out clean.   *Makes 8 servings*

Tip: To prepare in advance, bake the pudding as directed; cover and refrigerate up to one day. Before serving, microwave until heated through. Or, cover loosely with foil and bake in a preheated 325°F oven for about 20 minutes or until heated through. (Bring the dish to room temperature before placing it in a hot oven.)

Corn Pudding

Grilled Mesquite Vegetables

2 to 3 tablespoons MRS. DASH® Mesquite Grilling Blend

2 tablespoons olive oil, divided

1 eggplant, trimmed and cut into ½-inch slices

1 zucchini, quartered lengthwise

1 red onion, peeled and halved

2 red bell peppers, cut into large slices

2 green bell peppers, cut into large slices

1 tablespoon balsamic vinegar

Preheat barbecue grill to medium. In large bowl, combine Mrs. Dash® Mesquite Grilling Blend and 1 tablespoon olive oil. Add vegetables and toss until well coated. Place vegetables on grill. Cover and cook, turning vegetables once during cooking, until vegetables are tender and develop grill marks, about 3 to 4 minutes on each side. Remove vegetables from grill as soon as they are cooked. Coarsely chop vegetables into ½-inch pieces. Mix remaining olive oil and balsamic vinegar in large bowl. Add cut vegetables and toss to coat. Serve at room temperature. *Makes 6 servings*

NOTE: Grilling vegetables dehydrates them slightly and intensifies flavors while Mrs. Dash Mesquite Grilling Blend adds a third dimension of flavor. This dish makes a colorful accompaniment to any grilled meat.

Fast Pesto Focaccia

1 can (13.8 ounces) refrigerated pizza dough

2 tablespoons prepared pesto

4 sun-dried tomatoes (packed in oil), drained

1. Preheat oven to 425°F. Lightly grease 8-inch square baking pan. Unroll pizza dough. Fold in half; press gently into pan.

2. Spread pesto evenly over dough. Chop tomatoes or snip with kitchen scissors; sprinkle over pesto. Press tomatoes into dough. Using wooden spoon handle, make indentations in dough every 2 inches.

3. Bake 10 to 12 minutes or until golden brown. Cut into 16 squares. Serve warm or at room temperature. *Makes 16 servings*

Grilled Mesquite Vegetables

Mediterranean Pilaf

2 tablespoons I CAN'T BELIEVE IT'S NOT BUTTER!® Spread
1 cup uncooked converted rice
2½ cups chicken broth
¼ cup toasted pine nuts (optional)
3 tablespoons grated Parmesan cheese
2 tablespoons finely chopped fresh basil leaves
¼ teaspoon ground black pepper

In 3-quart saucepan, melt I Can't Believe It's Not Butter!® Spread over medium-high heat. Stir in uncooked rice and cook, stirring frequently, 2 minutes or until rice is golden. Add broth and bring to a boil over high heat. Reduce heat to low and simmer covered 20 minutes. Stir in pine nuts, Parmesan cheese, basil and pepper. Let stand covered 2 minutes. Stir before serving.   *Makes 4 servings*

NOTE: Recipe can be halved.

Mandarin Orange Mold

1¾ cups boiling water
2 packages (4-serving size each) orange flavor gelatin
3 cups ice cubes
1 can (15.25 ounces) DOLE® Tropical Mixed Fruit, drained
1 can (11 ounces) DOLE® Mandarin Oranges, drained

● Stir boiling water into gelatin in large bowl at least 2 minutes until completely dissolved. Add ice cubes. Stir until ice is melted and gelatin is thickened. Stir in fruit salad and mandarin oranges. Spoon into 6-cup mold.

● Refrigerate 4 hours or until firm. Unmold.* Garnish as desired.   *Makes 12 servings*

To unmold, dip mold in warm water about 15 seconds. Gently pull gelatin from around edges with moist fingers. Place moistened serving plate on top of mold. Invert mold and plate. Holding mold and plate together, shake slightly to loosen. Gently remove mold.

Prep Time: 15 minutes
Chill Time: 4 hours

Mediterranean Pilaf

Carrie's Sweet Potato Casserole

    Topping (recipe follows)
 3 **pounds sweet potatoes, cooked and peeled***
 ½ **cup (1 stick) butter, softened**
 ½ **cup granulated sugar**
 2 **eggs, beaten**
 ½ **cup evaporated milk**
 1 **teaspoon vanilla**
 1 **cup chopped pecans**

For faster preparation, substitute canned sweet potatoes.

1. Prepare Topping; set aside. Preheat oven to 350°F. Grease 8 (6-ounce) ovenproof ramekins or 13×9-inch baking dish.

2. Mash sweet potatoes and butter in large bowl. Beat with electric mixer at medium speed until light and fluffy. Add granulated sugar, eggs, evaporated milk and vanilla, beating after each addition. Spoon evenly into prepared ramekins. Spoon Topping over potatoes; sprinkle with pecans.

3. Bake 20 to 25 minutes or until set.   *Makes 8 servings*

TOPPING: Combine 1 cup packed light brown sugar, ½ cup all-purpose flour and ⅓ cup melted butter in medium bowl; mix well.

Honey and Vanilla Glazed Carrots

 ¼ **cup (½ stick) butter or margarine**
 ¼ **cup honey**
 1½ **pounds baby carrots (about 5 cups), cooked until crisp-tender**
 1½ **teaspoons WATKINS® Vanilla Extract**
    Pinch WATKINS® Ginger
    Salt and WATKINS® Black Pepper to taste

Melt butter in medium saucepan. Add honey and stir until blended. Add carrots, vanilla and ginger. Cook over low heat, stirring occasionally, until carrots are well glazed. Season with salt and pepper.   *Makes 10 servings (5 cups)*

Carrie's Sweet Potato Casserole

Prosciutto Provolone Rolls

1 loaf (1 pound) frozen bread dough, thawed
¼ cup garlic and herb spreadable cheese
6 thin slices prosciutto (about one 3-ounce package)
6 slices provolone cheese

1. Spray 12 standard (2¾-inch) muffin pan cups with nonstick cooking spray. Roll out dough on lightly floured surface to 12×10-inch rectangle.

2. Spread garlic and herb cheese evenly over dough. Arrange prosciutto slices over herb cheese; top with provolone slices. Starting with long side, roll up dough jelly-roll style; pinch seam to seal.

3. Cut crosswise into 12 slices; arrange slices cut sides down in prepared muffin cups. Cover and let rise in warm, draft-free place 30 to 40 minutes or until nearly doubled in bulk.

4. Preheat oven to 350°F. Bake rolls about 18 minutes or until golden brown. Loosen edges of rolls with knife; remove from pan to wire rack. Serve warm.   *Makes 12 rolls*

Vegetables & Wild Rice

2⅓ cups water
2 tablespoons butter or margarine
1 box UNCLE BEN'S® Long Grain & Wild Rice Roasted Garlic
1 cup corn, fresh or frozen
1 medium tomato, chopped
4 strips bacon, cooked and crumbled
3 tablespoons chopped green onions

COOK: CLEAN: Wash hands. In medium skillet, combine water, butter, rice and contents of seasoning packet. Bring to a boil. Cover tightly and simmer 15 minutes. Add corn and simmer 15 minutes or until water is absorbed. Stir in tomato and bacon. Sprinkle with green onions.

SERVE: Serve with garlic toast, if desired.

CHILL: Refrigerate leftovers immediately.   *Makes 6 servings*

Prosciutto Provolone Rolls

Potatoes au Gratin

4 to 6 medium unpeeled baking potatoes (about 2 pounds)

2 cups (8 ounces) shredded Cheddar cheese

1 cup (4 ounces) shredded Swiss cheese

2 tablespoons butter

3 tablespoons all-purpose flour

2½ cups milk

2 tablespoons Dijon mustard

¼ teaspoon salt

¼ teaspoon black pepper

1. Preheat oven to 400°F. Grease 13×9-inch baking dish.

2. Cut potatoes into thin slices. Layer potatoes in prepared dish. Top with cheeses.

3. Melt butter in medium saucepan over medium heat. Stir in flour; cook 1 minute. Stir in milk, mustard, salt and pepper; bring to a boil. Reduce heat; cook, stirring constantly, until mixture thickens. Pour milk mixture over cheese. Cover pan with foil.

4. Bake 30 minutes. Remove foil; bake 15 to 20 minutes or until potatoes are tender and top is brown. Let stand 10 minutes before serving.   *Makes 6 to 8 servings*

Orange Sesame Couscous

1 cup fresh orange juice (3 SUNKIST® oranges)

½ cup chopped red or green bell pepper

1 teaspoon sesame oil

⅛ teaspoon salt

⅔ cup uncooked couscous

1 SUNKIST® orange, peeled and cut into bite-size pieces

3 tablespoons chopped green onions

In medium saucepan, combine orange juice, bell pepper, sesame oil and salt. Bring just to a boil; stir in couscous. Cover and remove from heat. Let stand 5 minutes. Stir with fork to fluff up mixture. Stir in orange pieces and green onions.   *Makes 3 (1-cup) servings*

Potatoes au Gratin

Oven-Roasted Asparagus

1 bunch (12 to 14 ounces) asparagus spears

1 tablespoon olive oil

½ teaspoon salt

¼ teaspoon black pepper

¼ cup grated Asiago or Parmesan cheese

1. Preheat oven to 425°F.

2. Trim off and discard tough ends of asparagus spears. Peel stem ends with vegetable peeler, if desired. Arrange asparagus in shallow baking dish; drizzle with oil, turning to coat. Sprinkle with salt and pepper.

3. Roast asparagus until tender, about 12 to 18 minutes depending on thickness of asparagus. Sprinkle with cheese. *Makes 4 servings*

Savory Apple Roast

2 baking apples

2 sweet potatoes

2 Vidalia onions

1 tablespoon olive oil

2 teaspoons chopped garlic

1 tablespoon balsamic vinegar

Preheat oven to 450°F. Line roasting pan with aluminum foil. Core and cut apples into quarters. Cut sweet potatoes into 6 to 8 large pieces. Cut onions into small wedges. Combine apples, vegetables, olive oil and garlic. Roast in prepared pan 40 to 45 minutes or until sweet potatoes are tender. Sprinkle with balsamic vinegar before serving. Serve hot or cold.

Makes 6 servings

Prep Time: 10 minutes
Cook Time: 40 to 45 minutes

Favorite recipe from **New York Apple Association, Inc.**

Oven-Roasted Asparagus

Wild Rice, Cranberry and Apple Stuffing

1 tablespoon olive oil or butter

1 medium apple, diced (about 1 cup)

2 stalks celery, diced (about ⅔ cup)

1 clove garlic, minced

½ teaspoon dried thyme

½ teaspoon dried sage

1 cup hot cooked white or brown rice

1 cup hot cooked wild rice

½ cup orange juice

¼ cup dried cranberries

¼ cup sliced green onions

Salt and black pepper

1. Heat oil in large saucepan over medium-high heat. Add apple, celery and garlic; cook and stir 5 minutes or until softened.

2. Reduce heat to medium-low. Add thyme and sage; cook and stir 1 minute. Add white and wild rice, orange juice and cranberries; cook and stir 2 minutes until heated through. Just before serving, stir in green onions and season with salt and pepper to taste.

Makes 8 servings

SERVING SUGGESTION: Serve stuffing in baked acorn squash halves.

Mashed Maple Sweet Potatoes

3 cans (15 ounces each) PRINCELLA® or SUGARY SAM® Cut Sweet Potatoes, drained

4 tablespoons butter

¼ cup half-and-half

3 tablespoons maple syrup

Salt and black pepper to taste

Preheat oven to 350°F. In medium mixing bowl, combine all ingredients; blend with electric mixer or in food processor. Transfer mixture to greased 9-inch square casserole dish; smooth surface. Cover and bake for 30 minutes.

Makes 5 to 7 servings

Wild Rice, Cranberry and Apple Stuffing

Make it
CASUAL

Grilled Vegetable Pizza (page 138)

Veggie No Boiling Lasagna (page 146)

Stuffed Focaccia Sandwich (page 126)

Super-Moist Cornbread

1 package (8½ ounces) corn muffin mix

1 can (11 ounces) Mexican-style corn, drained

½ cup HELLMANN'S® or BEST FOODS® Real Mayonnaise

1 egg, slightly beaten

1. Preheat oven to 400°F. Spray 8-inch round cake pan with nonstick cooking spray; set aside.

2. In medium bowl, combine all ingredients until moistened. Evenly spread into prepared pan.

3. Bake 25 minutes or until toothpick inserted in center comes out clean.

Makes 8 servings

Prep Time: 5 minutes
Cook Time: 25 minutes

Stuffed Focaccia Sandwich

1 container (5.2 ounces) soft cheese with garlic and herbs

1 (10-inch) round herb or onion focaccia, cut in half horizontally

½ cup thinly sliced red onion

½ cup coarsely chopped green olives, drained

¼ cup sliced mild banana pepper

4 ounces thinly sliced deli hard salami

6 ounces thinly sliced oven-roasted turkey breast

1 package (⅔ ounce) fresh basil, stems removed

1. Spread soft cheese over both cut sides of focaccia. Layer bottom half evenly with remaining ingredients. Cover sandwich with top half of focaccia; press down firmly.

2. Cut sandwich into 4 equal pieces. Serve immediately or wrap individually in plastic wrap and refrigerate until needed.

Makes 4 servings

TIP: This sandwich is great for make-ahead lunches or picnics.

Super-Moist Cornbread

Manicotti

1 container (16 ounces) ricotta cheese

2 cups (8 ounces) shredded mozzarella cheese

½ cup cottage cheese

2 eggs, beaten

2 tablespoons grated Parmesan cheese

½ teaspoon minced garlic

  Salt and black pepper

1 package (about 8 ounces) uncooked manicotti shells

1 pound ground beef

1 jar (26 ounces) pasta sauce

2 cups water

1. Combine ricotta cheese, mozzarella cheese, cottage cheese, eggs, Parmesan cheese and garlic in large bowl; mix well. Season with salt and pepper.

2. Stuff cheese mixture into manicotti shells. Place filled shells in 13×9-inch baking dish. Preheat oven to 375°F.

3. Brown ground beef in large skillet over medium-high heat, stirring to break up meat; drain fat. Stir in pasta sauce and water (mixture will be thin). Pour sauce over filled manicotti shells.

4. Cover with foil; bake 1 hour or until sauce has thickened and shells are tender.

Makes 6 servings

Manicotti

Stuffed Crust Pizza

1 package (13.8 ounces) refrigerated pizza crust dough

7 mozzarella cheese sticks

¾ cup RAGÚ® Old World Style® Pasta Sauce

1 small red bell pepper, diced

1 cup shredded mozzarella cheese (about 4 ounces)

12 slices pepperoni

On greased baking sheet, roll pizza dough into 13×10-inch rectangle. Arrange 2 cheese sticks on each long edge, then 1½ cheese sticks on each shorter edge. Lift pizza dough over cheese sticks and press to seal tightly. Freeze 20 minutes.

Meanwhile, preheat oven to 425°F. Bake pizza dough 6 minutes. Evenly top with Pasta Sauce, red pepper, shredded cheese and pepperoni.

Bake 6 minutes or until cheese is melted and crust is golden.   *Makes 6 servings*

Prep Time: 10 minutes
Chill Time: 20 minutes
Cook Time: 15 minutes

Toasted Sun-Dried Tomato Bread

½ cup I CAN'T BELIEVE IT'S NOT BUTTER!® Spread

2 tablespoons finely chopped, drained sun-dried tomatoes packed in oil

1 shallot or small onion, finely chopped

1 clove garlic, finely chopped

1 loaf French or Italian bread (about 12 inches long), halved lengthwise

In small bowl, blend all ingredients except bread. Evenly spread bread with sun-dried tomato mixture. On baking sheet, arrange bread and broil until golden. Slice and serve.

Makes about 12 servings

Stuffed Crust Pizza

Best Beef Brisket Sandwich Ever

    1 beef brisket (about 3 pounds)
    2 cups apple cider, divided
 ⅓ cup chopped fresh thyme *or* 2 tablespoons dried thyme
    1 head garlic, cloves separated, peeled and crushed
    2 tablespoons whole black peppercorns
    1 tablespoon mustard seeds
    1 tablespoon Cajun seasoning
    1 teaspoon ground cumin
    1 teaspoon celery seeds
    1 teaspoon ground allspice
    2 to 4 whole cloves
    1 bottle (12 ounces) dark beer
 10 to 12 sourdough sandwich rolls, halved

SLOW COOKER DIRECTIONS

1. Place brisket, ½ cup apple cider, thyme, garlic, peppercorns, mustard seeds, Cajun seasoning, cumin, celery seeds, allspice and cloves in large resealable food storage bag. Seal bag; marinate in refrigerator overnight.

2. Place brisket and marinade in slow cooker. Add remaining 1½ cups apple cider and beer. Cover; cook on LOW 10 hours or until brisket is tender.

3. Slice brisket and place on sandwich rolls. Strain sauce; drizzle over meat.

Makes 10 to 12 servings

SERVING SUGGESTION: Serve the sandwiches with a mustard spread or horseradish sauce for extra flavor.

Best Beef Brisket Sandwich Ever

Italian Sausage Stew

8 ounces hot Italian turkey sausage, casings removed, or reduced-fat bulk pork
    sausage with ¼ teaspoon dried pepper flakes

1 green bell pepper

2 garlic cloves, minced

1 can (about 15 ounces) navy beans, rinsed and drained

1 can (about 14 ounces) Italian-style stewed tomatoes, undrained

1 cup reduced-sodium beef or chicken broth

1 teaspoon dried rosemary, crushed

Cook sausage, bell pepper and garlic in large saucepan over medium-high heat until
sausage is no longer pink, stirring to break up meat. Add beans, tomatoes, broth and
rosemary; bring to a simmer. Cover and simmer over medium-low heat 5 minutes or
until bell pepper is tender. *Makes 4 servings*

SERVING SUGGESTION: Serve with crusty Italian bread and a Caesar salad.

Bubbling Wisconsin Cheese Bread

½ cup (2 ounces) shredded Wisconsin Mozzarella cheese

⅓ cup mayonnaise or salad dressing

⅛ teaspoon garlic powder

⅛ teaspoon onion powder

1 loaf (16 ounces) French bread, halved lengthwise

⅓ cup (1 ounce) grated Wisconsin Parmesan cheese

Preheat oven to 350°F. Combine mozzarella cheese, mayonnaise, garlic powder and onion
powder in mixing bowl; mix well (mixture will be very thick). Spread half of mixture over each
bread half. Sprinkle with Parmesan cheese. Bake 20 to 25 minutes or until bubbly and lightly
browned.* Cut each half into 8 slices. *Makes 16 servings*

*To broil, position on rack 4 inches from heat for 3 to 5 minutes.

*Favorite recipe from **Wisconsin Milk Marketing Board***

Italian Sausage Stew

Chicken Parmesan Stromboli

1 pound boneless skinless chicken breast halves

½ **teaspoon salt**

¼ **teaspoon ground black pepper**

2 teaspoons olive oil

2 cups shredded mozzarella cheese (about 8 ounces)

1 jar (1 pound 10 ounces) RAGÚ® Chunky Pasta Sauce, divided

2 tablespoons grated Parmesan cheese

1 tablespoon finely chopped fresh parsley

1 pound fresh or thawed frozen bread dough

Preheat oven to 400°F. Season chicken with salt and pepper. In 12-inch skillet, heat olive oil over medium-high heat and brown chicken. Remove chicken from skillet and let cool; pull into large shreds.

In medium bowl, combine chicken, mozzarella cheese, ½ cup Pasta Sauce, Parmesan cheese and parsley; set aside.

On greased jelly-roll pan, press dough to form 12×10-inch rectangle. Arrange chicken mixture down center of dough. Cover filling with dough, bringing one long side into center, then overlapping with other long side. Pinch seam to seal. Fold in ends and pinch to seal. Arrange on pan, seam-side down. Gently press in sides to form 12×4-inch loaf. Bake 35 minutes or until dough is cooked and golden. Cut stromboli into slices. Heat remaining Pasta Sauce and serve with stromboli.   *Makes 6 servings*

Chicken Parmesan Stromboli

Grilled Vegetable Pizzas

2 tablespoons olive oil

1 clove garlic, minced

1 medium red bell pepper, halved and seeded

1 (½-inch-thick) slice red onion

2 (½-inch-thick) slices eggplant, lightly salted

4 small (6-inch) prebaked pizza crusts

4 teaspoons prepared pesto sauce

1¼ cups grated CABOT® Sharp Cheddar (about 5 ounces), divided

1. Preheat barbecue grill, allowing coals to turn to gray ash or setting gas grill to medium.

2. In small bowl, combine olive oil and garlic. Place vegetables on grill and cook, brushing with oil-garlic mixture and turning frequently, until lightly browned and tender, about 10 minutes.

3. Remove vegetables from grill, let cool slightly and cut into ½-inch pieces.

4. Place pizza crusts on grill, top-side down, and cook until warm, 3 to 5 minutes.

5. Remove crusts from grill and spread each with 1 teaspoon pesto sauce. Top each with ¼ cup cheese and one fourth of vegetables. Scatter remaining ¼ cup cheese on top.

6. Return pizzas to grill and cook until crust is crisp and cheese is melted. Cut pizzas into wedges and serve. *Makes 8 servings*

Grilled Vegetable Pizzas

Pressed Party Sandwich

1 loaf (about 12 inches) hearty peasant or sourdough bread

1 to 2 bunches fresh basil

6 ounces thinly sliced smoked provolone or mozzarella cheese (about 9 slices)

3 plum tomatoes, sliced

1 red onion, thinly sliced

2 roasted red bell peppers

2 to 3 tablespoons extra-virgin olive oil

1 tablespoon balsamic vinegar

¼ teaspoon salt

¼ teaspoon black pepper

1. Cut bread in half lengthwise. Place halves cut side up on work surface. Gently pull out some of interior, leaving at least 1½ inches bread shell.

2. Layer basil, cheese, tomatoes, onion and peppers on bottom half of loaf; drizzle with oil and vinegar. Season with salt and pepper; cover with top half of loaf.

3. Wrap loaf tightly in plastic wrap; place on baking sheet. Top with another baking sheet. Place canned goods or heavy pot or pan on top of baking sheet. Refrigerate sandwich several hours or overnight.

4. To serve, remove weights and plastic wrap from sandwich. Cut sandwich crosswise into 1-inch slices; arrange on serving platter. *Makes 12 slices*

Tip: To reduce the sharp flavor of the onion, place the slices in a sieve or colander and rinse with cold water for a few seconds. Shake the slices and pat dry before adding to the sandwich.

Pressed Party Sandwich

Spicy Hunan Ribs

1⅓ cups hoisin sauce or *Cattlemen's*® Golden Honey Barbecue Sauce

⅔ cup *Frank's*® *RedHot*® XTRA Hot Cayenne Pepper Sauce or *Frank's*® *RedHot*®
Cayenne Pepper Sauce

¼ cup soy sauce

2 tablespoons brown sugar

2 tablespoons dark sesame oil

2 tablespoons grated peeled ginger root

4 cloves garlic, crushed through a press

2 full racks pork spareribs, trimmed (about 6 pounds)

1. Combine hoisin sauce, XTRA Hot Sauce, soy sauce, brown sugar, sesame oil, ginger and garlic; mix well.

2. Place ribs into large resealable plastic food storage bags. Pour 1½ cups sauce mixture over ribs; refrigerate remaining sauce mixture. Seal bags and marinate in refrigerator 1 to 3 hours or overnight.

3. Prepare grill for indirect cooking over medium-low heat (250°F). Place ribs on rib rack or in foil pan; discard marinade. Cook on covered grill 2½ to 3 hours until very tender. Baste with remaining sauce during last 15 minutes of cooking. If desired, grill ribs over direct heat at end of cooking to char slightly. *Makes 4 to 6 servings*

TIP: Use Kansas City or St. Louis-style ribs for this recipe.

Prep Time: 5 minutes
Marinate Time: 1 hour
Cook Time: 3 hours

Spicy Hunan Ribs

Baked Black Bean Chili

1½ **pounds lean ground beef**

¼ **cup chopped sweet onion**

¼ **cup chopped green bell pepper**

1 **can (about 15 ounces) black beans, rinsed and drained**

1 **can (about 14 ounces) diced tomatoes with green chilies**

1 **can (about 14 ounces) beef broth**

1 **can (8 ounces) tomato sauce**

5 **tablespoons chili powder**

1 **tablespoon sugar**

1 **tablespoon ground cumin**

1 **teaspoon dried minced onion**

⅛ **teaspoon garlic powder**

⅛ **teaspoon ground ginger**

2 **cups (8 ounces) shredded Mexican cheese blend**

1. Preheat oven to 350°F. Cook beef, onion and bell pepper in large nonstick skillet over medium-high heat until meat is no longer pink, stirring to break up meat. Drain and transfer to 4-quart casserole.

2. Add remaining ingredients except cheese; stir until well blended. Cover and bake 30 minutes, stirring every 10 minutes. Uncover and top with cheese; bake about 5 minutes or until cheese begins to melt. *Makes 6 to 8 servings*

Baked Black Bean Chili

Veggie No Boiling Lasagna

1 tablespoon olive oil

1 medium sweet onion, thinly sliced

1 medium red bell pepper, thinly sliced

1 medium zucchini, cut in half lengthwise and thinly sliced

2 containers (15 ounces each) ricotta cheese

2 cups shredded mozzarella cheese (about 8 ounces), divided

½ cup grated Parmesan cheese, divided

2 eggs

2 jars (1 pound 10 ounces each) RAGÚ® Old World Style® Pasta Sauce

12 uncooked lasagna noodles

Preheat oven to 375°F. In 12-inch nonstick skillet, heat olive oil over medium-high heat and cook onion, red bell pepper and zucchini, stirring occasionally, 5 minutes or until softened.

Meanwhile, combine ricotta cheese, 1 cup mozzarella cheese, ¼ cup Parmesan cheese and eggs.

In 13×9-inch baking dish, spread 1 cup Pasta Sauce. Layer 4 uncooked noodles, then 1 cup Sauce, half of ricotta mixture and half of vegetables; repeat. Top with remaining uncooked noodles and 2 cups Sauce. Reserve remaining Sauce.

Cover with foil and bake 1 hour. Remove foil; sprinkle with remaining cheeses. Bake uncovered 10 minutes. Let stand 10 minutes before serving. Serve with reserved Pasta Sauce, heated.   *Makes 12 servings*

Prep Time: 15 minutes

Cook Time: 1 hour and 15 minutes

Veggie No Boiling Lasagna

Super-Sloppy Sloppy Joes with Broccoli Slaw

1½ **pounds ground beef (95% lean)**

½ **cup chopped onion**

¼ **teaspoon pepper**

½ **cup canned black beans, rinsed, drained**

½ **cup frozen corn**

½ **cup ketchup**

½ **cup prepared barbecue sauce**

6 **whole wheat sandwich buns, toasted**

BROCCOLI SLAW:

¼ **cup prepared reduced-fat ranch dressing**

1 **tablespoon Dijon-style mustard**

2 **cups packaged broccoli slaw**

1. Brown ground beef with onion in large nonstick skillet over medium heat 8 to 10 minutes or until beef is not pink, breaking up into ¾-inch crumbles. Season with pepper. Stir in beans, corn, ketchup and barbecue sauce. Cook 3 to 5 minutes or until heated through, stirring occasionally.

2. Meanwhile, prepare Broccoli Slaw. Combine dressing and mustard in medium bowl. Add broccoli slaw; toss to coat.

3. Place about ⅔ cup beef mixture on bottom half of each bun; top with ¼ cup Broccoli Slaw. Close sandwiches. *Makes 6 servings*

Prep and Cook Time: 30 minutes

*Favorite recipe from **National Cattlemen's Beef Association on behalf of The Beef Checkoff***

Super-Sloppy Sloppy Joes with Broccoli Slaw

German Potato Salad with Grilled Sausage

⅔ **cup prepared vinaigrette salad dressing**

¼ **cup** *French's®* **Spicy Brown Mustard or** *French's®* **Honey Dijon Mustard**

1 **tablespoon sugar**

1½ **pounds red or other boiling potatoes, cut into ¾-inch cubes**

1 **teaspoon salt**

1 **cup chopped green bell pepper**

1 **cup chopped celery**

½ **cup chopped onion**

½ **pound kielbasa or smoked sausage, split lengthwise**

1. Combine salad dressing, mustard and sugar in large bowl; set aside.

2. Place potatoes in large saucepan. Add salt and enough water to cover potatoes. Heat to boiling. Cook 10 to 15 minutes until potatoes are tender. Drain and transfer to bowl. Add bell pepper, celery and onion. Set aside.

3. Grill sausage over medium-high heat until lightly browned and heated through. Cut into small cubes. Add to bowl with potatoes. Toss well to coat evenly. Serve warm.

Makes 6 to 8 servings

TIP: For zesty baked beans, add ½ cup French's® Mustard to 2 (16-ounce) cans pork and beans. Heat and serve.

Prep Time: 15 minutes
Cook Time: 15 minutes

German Potato Salad with Grilled Sausage

Stuffed Pizza

2 loaves (1 pound each) frozen bread dough, thawed
1 bottle (15 ounces) CONTADINA® Pizza Squeeze Pizza Sauce, divided
1 package (3 ounces) sliced pepperoni, quartered
1 package (10 ounces) frozen chopped spinach, thawed and squeezed dry
1 cup (4 ounces) shredded mozzarella cheese
1 carton (8 ounces) ricotta cheese
1 cup grated Parmesan cheese
1 can (3.8 ounces) sliced ripe olives, drained
1 tablespoon olive oil
1 tablespoon grated Parmesan cheese

1. Roll bread dough into two 12-inch circles on floured surface. Place one circle on greased baking sheet.

2. Spread with ¼ cup pizza sauce to 1 inch from edge.

3. Combine pepperoni, spinach, mozzarella, ricotta, 1 cup Parmesan cheese and olives in large bowl. Spread mixture over pizza sauce. Squeeze ¼ cup pizza sauce evenly over filling; dampen outside edge. Place remaining bread dough on top and seal. Cut 8 steam vents.

4. Bake on lowest rack in preheated 350°F oven for 20 minutes. Brush with olive oil; sprinkle with 1 tablespoon Parmesan cheese.

5. Bake for additional 15 to 20 minutes or until well browned. Let stand 15 minutes before cutting. Warm remaining pizza sauce and serve over wedges of pizza.   *Makes 8 servings*

Prep Time: 20 minutes
Cook Time: 40 minutes
Stand Time: 15 minutes

Stuffed Pizza

Breakfast &
BRUNCH

Individual Spinach & Bacon Quiches (page 180)

Apricot Mini Muffins (page 174)

Smoked Salmon Hash Browns (page 156)

Tortilla Scramble with Salsa

  8 **eggs**

¼ **cup heavy whipping cream or half and half**

  1 **tablespoon butter**

  3 **tablespoons ORTEGA® Salsa, any variety**

  1 **cup broken ORTEGA Taco Shells**

½ **cup Cheddar cheese, grated**

    Tortilla chips, chopped parsley and salsa (optional)

COMBINE eggs and heavy cream in mixing bowl. Beat with wire whisk.

MELT butter in heavy skillet. Add egg mixture and stir in 3 tablespoons salsa. Scramble eggs until they begin to set. Add broken taco shells and cheese, stirring to mix.

DIVIDE egg mixture and place on individual plates.

TOP with tortilla chips, parsley and salsa, if desired.

Makes 4 servings

Smoked Salmon Hash Browns

  3 **cups frozen hash brown potatoes, thawed**

  2 **pouches (3 ounces each) smoked Pacific salmon***

½ **cup chopped onion**

½ **cup chopped bell pepper**

¼ **teaspoon black pepper**

  2 **tablespoons vegetable oil**

*Smoked salmon in foil packages can be found in the canned fish section of the supermarket. Do not substitute lox or other fresh smoked salmon.

1. Combine potatoes, salmon, onion, bell pepper and black pepper in large bowl; mix well.

2. Heat oil in large nonstick skillet over medium-high heat. Add potato mixture; spread to cover surface of skillet. Carefully pat down to avoid oil spatter.

3. Cook 5 minutes or until crisp and browned. Turn over in large pieces. Cook 2 to 3 minutes or until brown.

Makes 4 servings

Tortilla Scramble with Salsa

Caramel-Nut Sticky Biscuits

TOPPING

⅔ **cup firmly packed brown sugar**

¼ **cup light corn syrup**

¼ **cup (½ stick) margarine, melted**

½ **teaspoon ground cinnamon**

1 **cup pecan halves**

BISCUITS

2 **cups all-purpose flour**

1 **cup QUAKER® Oats (quick or old fashioned, uncooked)**

¼ **cup granulated sugar**

1 **tablespoon baking powder**

¾ **teaspoon baking soda**

½ **teaspoon salt (optional)**

½ **teaspoon ground cinnamon**

⅓ **cup (5⅓ tablespoons) margarine**

1 **cup buttermilk***

*Sour milk can be substituted for buttermilk. For 1 cup sour milk, combine 1 tablespoon vinegar or lemon juice and enough milk to make 1 cup; let stand 5 minutes.

Heat oven to 425°F. For topping, combine first four ingredients; mix well. Spread onto bottom of 9-inch square baking pan. Sprinkle with pecans; set aside. For biscuits, combine dry ingredients; mix well. Cut in margarine with pastry blender or two knives until crumbly. Stir in buttermilk, mixing just until moistened. Knead gently on lightly floured surface 5 to 7 times; pat into 8-inch square. Cut with knife into sixteen 2-inch square biscuits; place over topping in pan. Bake 25 to 28 minutes or until golden brown. Let stand 3 minutes; invert onto large platter. Serve warm.
Makes 16 servings

Caramel-Nut Sticky Biscuits

Bratwurst Skillet

1½ pounds red potatoes

3 bratwurst links (about ¾ pound)

2 tablespoons butter

1½ teaspoons caraway seeds

4 cups shredded red cabbage

1. Cut potatoes into ¼- to ½-inch pieces; place in microwavable casserole. Microwave, covered, at HIGH 3 minutes; stir. Microwave 2 minutes more or until just tender.

2. Meanwhile, cut sausage into ¼-inch slices. Cook sausage in large heavy skillet over medium-high heat 8 minutes or until browned and no longer pink in center. Remove from pan with slotted spoon; set aside. Pour off drippings.

3. Melt butter in same skillet. Add potatoes and caraway seeds; cook, stirring occasionally, 6 to 8 minutes or until potatoes are golden and tender. Return sausage to skillet. Stir in cabbage; cover and cook 3 minutes or until cabbage is slightly wilted. Uncover and cook, stirring occasionally, 3 to 4 minutes or until cabbage is just tender yet still bright red.

Makes 4 servings

Breakfast Hash

1 pound BOB EVANS® Special Seasonings or Savory Sage Roll Sausage

2 cups chopped potatoes

¼ cup chopped red and/or green bell pepper

2 tablespoons chopped onion

6 eggs

2 tablespoons milk

Crumble sausage into large skillet. Add potatoes, pepper and onion. Cook over low heat until sausage is browned and potatoes are fork-tender, stirring occasionally. Drain off any drippings. Whisk eggs and milk in small bowl until blended. Add to sausage mixture; scramble until eggs are set but not dry. Serve hot. Refrigerate leftovers.   *Makes 6 to 8 servings*

SERVING SUGGESTION: Serve with fresh fruit.

Bratwurst Skillet

Morning Muffins with Blueberries

½ **cup plus 1 tablespoon sugar, divided**

⅛ **teaspoon ground cinnamon**

1¾ **cups all-purpose flour**

2 **teaspoons baking powder**

½ **teaspoon salt**

½ **cup milk**

¼ **cup vegetable oil**

1 **egg**

1 **teaspoon vanilla**

1 **teaspoon grated orange peel**

1 **cup fresh or frozen blueberries, thawed and dried**

1. Preheat oven to 400°F. Grease 12 standard (2½-inch) muffin pan cups or line with paper baking cups. Combine 1 tablespoon sugar and cinnamon in small bowl; set aside.

2. Combine flour, remaining ½ cup sugar, baking powder and salt in large bowl. Beat milk, oil, egg, vanilla and orange peel in small bowl until blended. Make well in center of flour mixture; stir in milk mixture just until moistened. Fold in blueberries. Spoon evenly into prepared muffin cups, filling about two-thirds full.

3. Bake 15 to 18 minutes or until toothpick inserted into centers comes out clean. Immediately sprinkle reserved sugar mixture over hot muffins. Transfer to wire racks. Serve warm.

Makes 12 muffins

Tip: For muffins with larger tops, fill the muffin cups almost full and bake at 400°F until a toothpick inserted into the centers comes out clean. Proceed as directed above. (The recipe will make about 8 big-top muffins.)

Morning Muffins with Blueberries

Delicious Ham & Cheese Puff Pie

2 cups (about 1 pound) diced cooked ham

1 package (10 ounces) frozen chopped spinach, thawed and squeezed dry

½ cup diced red bell pepper

4 green onions, sliced

3 eggs

¾ cup all-purpose flour

¾ cup (3 ounces) shredded Swiss cheese

¾ cup milk

1 tablespoon prepared mustard

1 teaspoon grated lemon peel

1 teaspoon dried dill weed

½ teaspoon garlic salt

½ teaspoon black pepper

Fresh dill sprigs and lemon slices (optional)

1. Preheat oven to 425°F. Grease round 2-quart casserole.

2. Combine ham, spinach, bell pepper and green onions in prepared casserole.

3. Beat eggs in medium bowl. Stir in flour, cheese, milk, mustard, lemon peel, dried dill, garlic salt and black pepper; mix well. Pour over ham mixture in casserole.

4. Bake 30 to 35 minutes or until puffed and browned. Cut into wedges; garnish with fresh dill and lemon slices.

Makes 4 to 6 servings

Delicious Ham & Cheese Puff Pie

Banana-Nut Buttermilk Waffles

¾ **cup walnuts or pecans**

2 **cups all-purpose flour**

2 **teaspoons baking powder**

1 **teaspoon salt**

2 **cups buttermilk**

2 **very ripe bananas, mashed (about 1 cup)**

5 **tablespoons butter, melted**

2 **eggs, separated**

¼ **cup sugar**

1 **teaspoon vanilla**

  Syrup, banana slices and nuts (optional)

1. Lightly spray waffle iron with nonstick cooking spray; preheat according to manufacturer's directions.

2. Toast walnuts in medium nonstick skillet over medium heat 5 to 8 minutes or until fragrant. Immediately transfer to plate to cool; chop and set aside.

3. Sift flour, baking powder and salt into medium bowl. Combine buttermilk, mashed bananas, butter, egg yolks, sugar, vanilla and walnuts in large bowl; mix well. Beat egg whites in medium bowl with electric mixer at high speed until stiff. Fold flour mixture into buttermilk mixture just until moistened. Fold in egg whites.

4. Pour ¾ cup batter into waffle iron and bake 4 to 6 minutes or until golden. Repeat with remaining batter. Serve with syrup, banana slices and nuts, if desired.   *Makes 4 servings*

Tip: If you don't have buttermilk, you can substitute soured fresh milk. Place 2 tablespoons lemon juice or distilled white vinegar in a measuring cup and add enough milk to measure 2 cups. Stir, then let the mixture stand at room temperature for 5 minutes.

Banana-Nut Buttermilk Waffles

Sunny Day Breakfast Burrito

    1 tablespoon butter
    ½ cup red or green bell pepper, chopped
    2 green onions, sliced
    6 eggs
    2 tablespoons milk
    ¼ teaspoon salt
    4 (7-inch) flour tortillas, warmed
    ½ cup (2 ounces) shredded colby-Jack or Mexican blend cheese
    ½ cup salsa

1. Melt butter in medium skillet over medium heat. Add bell pepper and green onions; cook and stir 3 minutes or until tender.

2. Beat eggs, milk and salt in medium bowl. Add egg mixture to skillet; reduce heat to low. Cook, stirring gently, until eggs are just set. (Eggs should be soft with no liquid remaining.)

3. Spoon one fourth of egg mixture down center of each tortilla; top with cheese. Fold in sides to enclose filling. Serve with salsa.   *Makes 4 servings*

Honey Roasted Ham Biscuits

    1 (10-ounce) can refrigerated buttermilk biscuits
    2 cups (12 ounces) diced HORMEL® CURE 81® ham
    ½ cup honey mustard
    ¼ cup finely chopped honey roasted peanuts, divided

Heat oven to 400°F. Separate biscuits. Place in muffin pan cups, pressing gently into bottoms and up sides of cups. In bowl, combine ham, honey mustard and 2 tablespoons peanuts. Spoon ham mixture evenly into biscuit cups. Sprinkle with remaining 2 tablespoons peanuts. Bake 15 to 17 minutes.   *Makes 10 servings*

Sunny Day Breakfast Burrito

Southwestern Sausage Drop Biscuits

1 pound BOB EVANS® Zesty Hot Roll Sausage

3 cups all-purpose (biscuit) baking mix

1¼ cups (5 ounces) shredded sharp Cheddar cheese

1 cup seeded diced fresh or drained canned tomatoes

1 cup chopped green onions

1 cup milk

¼ teaspoon paprika

Dash cayenne pepper

Butter (optional)

Preheat oven to 350°F. Crumble and cook sausage in medium skillet until browned. Drain on paper towels. Combine sausage and remaining ingredients except butter in large bowl; mix well. Shape dough into 2-inch balls; place on ungreased baking sheet. Bake 12 minutes or until golden. Serve hot with butter, if desired. Refrigerate leftovers.

Makes about 2 dozen small biscuits

Swiss Onion Potatoes Rosti

1 tablespoon olive oil

5 cups shredded fresh or frozen potatoes

1⅓ cups *French's*® French Fried Onions

1 cup (4 ounces) shredded Swiss or Cheddar cheese

½ cup crumbled cooked bacon

Applesauce or sour cream (optional)

1. Heat oil in 10-inch nonstick skillet over medium-high heat. Add potatoes, French Fried Onions, cheese and bacon. Cook 8 minutes or until lightly browned on bottom.

2. Loosen mixture and gently invert onto large serving platter. Return to skillet and cook 6 minutes or until browned.

3. Remove to serving platter. Season to taste with salt and pepper. If desired, serve with dollop of applesauce or sour cream on the side. *Makes 4 to 6 servings*

Southwestern Sausage Drop Biscuits

Cornmeal Pancakes with Blueberries

1½ **cups yellow cornmeal**

¾ **cup flour**

1½ **teaspoons baking powder**

1 **teaspoon salt**

2 **cups buttermilk**

2 **eggs, lightly beaten**

¼ **cup sugar**

2 **tablespoons butter, melted**

1 **cup frozen blueberries, slightly thawed,** *or* 4 **ounces fresh blueberries**

2 **teaspoons flour**

1. Mix cornmeal, flour, baking powder and salt in medium bowl.

2. Combine buttermilk, eggs, sugar and butter in large bowl; mix well. Fold cornmeal mixture into buttermilk mixture. Let stand 5 minutes.

3. Meanwhile, toss slightly thawed blueberries in flour. (If using fresh blueberries, omit this step.)

4. Spray griddle or large skillet with nonstick cooking spray; place over medium heat. Pour ⅓ cup batter per pancake onto griddle; sprinkle with blueberries. Cook 3 minutes or until golden on bottom; turn and cook 2 minutes or until golden. Serve immediately or place in warm oven while repeating with remaining batter. *Makes 4 servings*

Cornmeal Pancakes with Blueberries

Apricot Mini Muffins

1½ **cups all-purpose flour**

½ **cup sugar**

½ **cup finely chopped dried apricots**

¼ **teaspoon baking powder**

¼ **teaspoon baking soda**

⅛ **teapoon salt**

Pinch ground nutmeg

½ **cup (1 stick) butter, melted and cooled to room temperature**

2 **eggs**

2 **tablespoons milk**

1 **teaspoon vanilla**

1. Preheat oven to 350°F. Spray 24 mini (1¾-inch) muffin pan cups with nonstick cooking spray.

2. Blend flour, sugar, apricots, baking powder, baking soda, salt and nutmeg in large bowl. Whisk butter, eggs, milk and vanilla in small bowl. Add butter mixture to flour mixture; mix just until blended. Spoon about 1 tablespoon batter into each muffin cup. Bake 12 to 15 minutes or until toothpick inserted into centers comes out clean.   *Makes 2 dozen mini muffins*

Breakfast Pizza

1 **can (13.8 ounces) refrigerated pizza dough**

1 **package (7 ounces) fully cooked sausage patties, thawed, cut into ½-inch pieces**

3 **eggs**

½ **cup milk**

1 **teaspoon Italian seasoning**

2 **cups (8 ounces) shredded Italian-blend cheese**

1. Preheat oven to 425°F. Unroll pizza dough; pat onto bottom and up side of greased 12-inch pizza pan. Bake 5 minutes or until set but not browned.

2. Meanwhile, whisk eggs, milk and Italian seasoning in small bowl until well blended. Sprinkle sausage pieces over crust; top with cheese. Carefully pour egg mixture over cheese. Bake 15 to 20 minutes or until eggs are set and crust is golden.   *Makes 6 servings*

Apricot Mini Muffins

Stuffed French Toast with Fresh Berry Topping

2 cups mixed fresh berries (strawberries, raspberries, blueberries and/or blackberries)

2 tablespoons granulated sugar

⅔ cup lowfat ricotta cheese

¼ cup strawberry preserves

3 large eggs

⅔ cup (5 fluid-ounce can) NESTLÉ® CARNATION® Evaporated Fat Free Milk

2 tablespoons packed brown sugar

2 teaspoons vanilla extract

12 slices (about ¾-inch-thick) French bread

1 tablespoon vegetable oil, butter or margarine

Powdered sugar (optional)

Maple syrup, heated (optional)

COMBINE berries and granulated sugar in small bowl. Combine ricotta cheese and strawberry preserves in another small bowl; mix well. Combine eggs, evaporated milk, brown sugar and vanilla extract in pie plate or shallow bowl; mix well.

SPREAD ricotta-preserve mixture evenly over *6 slices* of bread. Top with *remaining* slices of bread to form sandwiches.

HEAT vegetable oil in large, nonstick skillet or griddle over medium heat. Dip sandwiches in egg mixture, coating both sides. Cook on each side for about 2 minutes or until golden brown.

SPRINKLE with powdered sugar; top with berries. Serve with maple syrup, if desired.

Makes 6 servings

Stuffed French Toast with Fresh Berry Topping

Peach Streusel Coffee Cake

2½ **cups biscuit baking mix, divided**

⅔ **cup whole milk**

1 **egg**

¼ **cup granulated sugar**

1 **teaspoon ground cinnamon**

1 **teaspoon vanilla extract**

1 **pound frozen unsweetened peaches, thawed and diced**

½ **cup packed dark brown sugar**

½ **cup pecan pieces**

3 **tablespoons cold unsalted butter, diced**

1. Preheat oven to 375°F. Spray 9-inch square baking pan with nonstick cooking spray.

2. For coffeecake, place 2 cups baking mix in medium bowl; break up lumps with spoon. Add milk, egg, granulated sugar, cinnamon and vanilla; stir until well blended. Add peaches; stir just until blended. Pour batter into prepared pan.

3. For topping, combine remaining ½ cup baking mix and brown sugar in small bowl; stir until well blended. Add pecans and butter; toss gently (do not break up small pieces of butter). Sprinkle evenly over batter.

4. Bake 35 minutes or until toothpick inserted into center comes out clean. Cool in pan on wire rack 15 minutes. Serve warm or at room temperature. *Makes 9 servings*

Peach Streusel Coffee Cake

Individual Spinach & Bacon Quiches

 3 slices bacon

½ small onion, diced

 1 package (10 ounces) frozen chopped spinach, thawed, drained and squeezed dry

½ teaspoon black pepper

⅛ teaspoon ground nutmeg

 Pinch salt

 1 container (15 ounces) whole milk ricotta cheese

 2 cups (8 ounces) shredded mozzarella cheese

 1 cup grated Parmesan cheese

 3 eggs, lightly beaten

1. Preheat oven to 350°F. Spray 10 standard (2½-inch) muffin pan cups with nonstick cooking spray.

2. Cook bacon in large skillet over medium-high heat until crisp. Drain on paper towels. Let bacon cool; crumble.

3. Add onion to same skillet; cook 5 minutes or until tender. Add spinach, pepper, nutmeg and salt; cook and stir over medium heat about 3 minutes or until liquid evaporates. Remove from heat. Stir in bacon; let mixture cool slightly.

4. Combine ricotta, mozzarella and Parmesan cheeses in large bowl. Add eggs; stir until well blended. Stir in cooled spinach mixture.

5. Divide mixture evenly among prepared muffin cups. Bake 40 minutes or until filling is set. Let stand 10 minutes. Run thin knife around edges to release. Serve hot or refrigerate and serve cold. *Makes 10 servings*

Individual Spinach & Bacon Quiches

Breakfast Empanadas

½ **pound bacon (about 10 slices)**

1 **package (15 ounces) refrigerated pie crusts (2 crusts)**

9 **eggs, divided**

1 **teaspoon water**

1 **teaspoon salt**

  Dash black pepper

1 **tablespoon butter**

2 **cups (8 ounces) Mexican-style shredded cheese, divided**

4 **tablespoons salsa**

1. Preheat oven to 425°F. Spray baking sheet with nonstick cooking spray. Cook bacon in large skillet over medium-high heat until crisp; drain on paper towels and wipe out skillet. Chop bacon into ¼-inch pieces. Cut pie crusts in half to make 4 semicircles; place on prepared baking sheet.

2. Beat 1 egg and water in small bowl; set aside. Beat remaining 8 eggs, salt and pepper in medium bowl until well blended. Heat same skillet over medium heat. Add butter; tilt skillet to coat bottom. Sprinkle bacon evenly over bottom of skillet. Pour eggs into skillet and cook 2 minutes without stirring. Gently stir until eggs form large curds and are still slightly moist. Transfer to plate to cool.

3. Spoon one fourth of cooled scrambled egg mixture onto half of each semicircle of dough. Reserve ¼ cup cheese; sprinkle remaining cheese over eggs. Top with salsa.

4. Brush inside edges of each semicircle with reserved egg-water mixture. Fold dough over top of egg mixture and seal edges with fork, making 4 empanadas. (Flour fork tines to prevent sticking, if necessary.)

5. Brush tops of empanadas with remaining egg-water mixture and sprinkle with reserved cheese. Bake 15 to 20 minutes or until golden.   *Makes 4 servings*

SERVING SUGGESTION: These empanadas are great for dinner, too. They can be prepared early in the day and reheated in a preheated 350°F oven for 20 to 25 minutes.

Breakfast Empanada

Dinner Party
DESSERTS

Double Cherry Crumbles (page 210)

Cranberry Pound Cake (page 204)

Apple Crunch Pie (page 186)

Heavenly Chocolate Mousse Pie

4 (1-ounce) squares unsweetened chocolate, melted
1 (14-ounce) can EAGLE BRAND® Sweetened Condensed Milk (NOT evaporated milk)
1½ teaspoons vanilla extract
1 cup (½ pint) whipping cream, whipped
1 (6-ounce) prepared chocolate crumb pie crust

1. In large bowl, beat chocolate with EAGLE BRAND® and vanilla until well blended.

2. Chill 15 minutes or until cooled; stir until smooth. Fold in whipped cream.

3. Pour into crust. Chill thoroughly. Garnish as desired. Store leftovers covered in refrigerator.
Makes 1 pie

Apple Crunch Pie

1 refrigerated pie crust (half of 15-ounce package)
1¼ cups all-purpose flour, divided
1 cup granulated sugar
6 tablespoons butter, melted, divided
1½ teaspoons ground cinnamon, divided
¾ teaspoon ground nutmeg, divided
½ teaspoon ground ginger
¼ teaspoon salt
4 cups diced peeled apples
½ cup packed brown sugar
½ cup chopped walnuts

1. Preheat oven to 350°F. Place dough in 9-inch pie pan; flute edge as desired.

2. Combine ¼ cup flour, granulated sugar, 2 tablespoons butter, 1 teaspoon cinnamon, ½ teaspoon nutmeg, ginger and salt. Add apples; toss to coat. Place apple mixture in crust.

3. Combine remaining 1 cup flour, 4 tablespoons butter, ½ teaspoon cinnamon, ¼ teaspoon nutmeg, brown sugar and walnuts in small bowl. Sprinkle evenly over apple mixture.

4. Bake 45 to 55 minutes or until apples are tender.
Makes 8 servings

Heavenly Chocolate Mousse Pie

Triple Chocolate Cake

1½ **cups sugar**

¾ **cup (1½ sticks) butter, softened**

1 **egg**

1 **teaspoon vanilla**

2 **cups all-purpose flour**

⅔ **cup unsweetened cocoa powder**

2 **teaspoons baking soda**

¼ **teaspoon salt**

1 **cup buttermilk**

¾ **cup sour cream**

    Chocolate Ganache Filling (recipe follows)

    Easy Chocolate Frosting (recipe follows)

1. Preheat oven to 350°F. Grease and flour two 9-inch round cake pans. Beat sugar and butter in large bowl with electric mixer at medium speed until light and fluffy. Beat in egg and vanilla until blended. Combine flour, cocoa, baking soda and salt in medium bowl; add to butter mixture alternately with buttermilk and sour cream, beginning and ending with flour mixture. Beat well after each addition. Divide batter evenly between prepared pans.

2. Bake 30 to 35 minutes or until toothpick inserted into centers comes out clean. Cool in pans 10 minutes. Remove from pans; cool completely on wire racks. Cut each cake layer in half horizontally.

3. Meanwhile, prepare filling and frosting. Place one cake layer on serving plate. Spread with one third of filling. Repeat layers two more times. Top with remaining cake layer. Spread frosting over top and side of cake. *Makes 12 to 16 servings*

CHOCOLATE GANACHE FILLING: Bring ¾ cup whipping cream, 1 tablespoon butter and 1 tablespoon granulated sugar to a boil; stir until sugar is dissolved. Place 1½ cups semisweet chocolate chips in medium bowl; pour cream mixture over chocolate and let stand 5 minutes. Stir until smooth; let stand 15 minutes or until desired consistency. (Filling will thicken as it cools.) Makes about 1½ cups.

EASY CHOCOLATE FROSTING: Beat ½ cup (1 stick) softened butter in large bowl with electric mixer at medium speed until creamy. Add 4 cups powdered sugar and ¾ cup cocoa alternately with ½ cup milk; beat until smooth. Stir in 1½ teaspoons vanilla. Makes about 3 cups.

Triple Chocolate Cake

Pear and Cranberry Cobbler

BISCUIT TOPPING

1 cup all-purpose flour

2 tablespoons sugar

2 teaspoons baking powder

¼ teaspoon salt

¼ cup (½ stick) butter, cut in chunks

½ cup milk

FILLING

4 cups diced peeled ripe pears (3 to 4 medium pears)

2 cups fresh cranberries

½ cup sugar

3 tablespoons all-purpose flour

¼ teaspoon ground cinnamon

2 tablespoons butter (optional)

1. Preheat oven to 375°F. Lightly grease 10-inch baking dish.

2. For topping, combine flour, sugar, baking powder and salt in medium bowl. Cut in butter with pastry blender or two knives until mixture forms coarse crumbs. Stir in milk until soft, sticky dough forms; set aside.

3. For filling, combine pears, cranberries, sugar, flour and cinnamon; stir gently. Spoon into prepared baking dish. Dot with butter, if desired. Drop dough by tablespoonfuls onto filling. Place baking dish on baking sheet; bake 25 to 35 minutes or until topping is golden and filling is bubbling. Serve warm.

Makes 6 to 8 servings

Pear and Cranberry Cobbler

Apple-Walnut Glazed Spice Baby Cakes

1 package (about 18 ounces) spice cake mix

1⅓ cups plus 3 tablespoons water, divided

3 eggs

⅓ cup vegetable oil

½ teaspoon vanilla

¾ cup chopped walnuts

12 ounces Granny Smith apples, peeled and cut into ½-inch cubes

¼ teaspoon ground cinnamon

1 jar (12 ounces) caramel ice cream topping

1. Preheat oven to 350°F. Lightly grease and flour 12 (1-cup) mini bundt pans.

2. Beat cake mix, 1⅓ cups water, eggs, oil and vanilla in large bowl with electric mixer at low speed 30 seconds. Beat at medium speed 2 minutes.

3. Spoon batter evenly into prepared pans. Bake 25 minutes or until toothpick inserted near centers comes out almost clean. Cool in pans on wire racks 15 minutes. Carefully invert cakes from pans onto wire racks; cool completely.

4. Meanwhile, heat large skillet over medium high heat. Add walnuts; cook 3 minutes or until nuts are lightly browned, stirring frequently. Remove nuts to small bowl. Combine apples, remaining 3 tablespoons water and cinnamon in same skillet; cook and stir over medium-high heat 3 minutes or until apples are crisp-tender. Remove from heat; stir in toasted walnuts and caramel topping. Spoon glaze over each cake.   *Makes 12 cakes*

Apple-Walnut Glazed Spice Baby Cakes

Lemony Blueberry Cheese Tart

1 (9-inch) frozen pie crust, thawed

1 (8-ounce) container mascarpone cheese or 1 (8-ounce) package cream cheese, softened

5 tablespoons lemon curd,* divided

2 cups fresh blueberries

*Lemon curd can be found in the jam and jelly section of the supermarket.

Preheat oven to 375°F. Press pie crust into 9-inch tart pan with removable bottom or leave in original aluminum pie tin. With tines of fork, pierce bottom and side. Bake until lightly browned, about 10 minutes. Refrigerate until cool, about 10 minutes. In small bowl, stir together cheese and 3 tablespoons lemon curd until smooth. (If mixture is too thick to spread, stir in small amount of milk.) Spread mixture in bottom of cooled tart shell. In medium bowl, gently stir blueberries and remaining 2 tablespoons lemon curd until thoroughly combined. Spoon blueberry mixture evenly over mascarpone layer. Cover and chill 2 hours. To serve, remove side of tart pan if used. Cut into wedges.   *Makes 8 servings*

Favorite recipe from **US Highbush Blueberry Council**

Sweet Potato Pie

2 eggs

1 can (15 ounces) PRINCELLA® or SUGARY SAM® Cut Sweet Potatoes, drained

1 can (12 ounces) evaporated milk

¾ cup sugar

1 teaspoon ground cinnamon

½ teaspoon ground ginger

¼ teaspoon ground cloves

1 unbaked 9-inch pie crust

Preheat oven to 425°F. In large mixing bowl, beat eggs. Add sweet potatoes and mix with electric hand mixer for 3 minutes until very smooth. Stir in evaporated milk and mix 2 minutes or until well blended. Add sugar, cinnamon, ginger and cloves; mix well. Pour mixture into pie crust and bake 15 minutes. Reduce temperature to 350°F and bake 40 to 50 minutes or until knife inserted near center comes out clean. Cool for 2 hours. Serve immediately or refrigerate. Serve with whipped topping or vanilla ice cream.   *Makes 8 servings*

Lemony Blueberry Cheese Tart

Carrot Snack Cake

1 package (about 18 ounces) butter recipe yellow cake mix with pudding in the mix, plus ingredients to prepare mix

2 jars (4 ounces each) strained carrot baby food

1½ cups chopped walnuts, divided

1 cup shredded carrots

½ cup golden raisins

1½ teaspoons ground cinnamon

1½ teaspoons vanilla, divided

1 package (8 ounces) cream cheese, softened

Grated peel of 1 lemon

2 teaspoons fresh lemon juice

3 cups powdered sugar

1. Preheat oven to 350°F. Grease 13×9-inch baking pan.

2. Prepare cake mix according to package directions but use only ½ cup water instead of amount called for in directions. Stir carrot baby food, 1 cup walnuts, carrots, raisins, cinnamon and ½ teaspoon vanilla into batter. Spread in prepared pan.

3. Bake 40 minutes or until cake begins to pull away from sides of pan and toothpick inserted into center comes out clean. Cool completely in pan on wire rack.

4. Beat cream cheese in large bowl with electric mixer at medium speed until fluffy. Beat in lemon peel, lemon juice and remaining 1 teaspoon vanilla. Gradually add powdered sugar, scraping down side of bowl occasionally; beat until well blended and smooth. Spread frosting over cooled cake; sprinkle with remaining ½ cup walnuts. Refrigerate 2 hours before cutting.

Makes 24 servings

Carrot Snack Cake

Mom's Pumpkin Pie

1½ **cans (15 ounces each) solid-pack pumpkin**
1 **can (12 ounces) evaporated milk**
1 **cup sugar**
2 **eggs**
2 **tablespoons maple syrup**
1 **teaspoon ground cinnamon**
1 **teaspoon vanilla**
½ **teaspoon salt**
2 **(9-inch) unbaked pie shells**
   Whipped cream (optional)

1. Preheat oven to 350°F. Combine pumpkin, evaporated milk, sugar, eggs, maple syrup, cinnamon, vanilla and salt in large bowl; mix well. Divide mixture evenly between pie shells.

2. Place pie pans on baking sheet. Bake 1 hour or until toothpick inserted into centers comes out clean. Cool completely. Top with whipped cream.   *Makes 2 (9-inch) pies*

Bananas Foster

6 **tablespoons I CAN'T BELIEVE IT'S NOT BUTTER!® Spread**
3 **tablespoons firmly packed brown sugar**
4 **ripe medium bananas, sliced diagonally**
2 **tablespoons dark rum or brandy (optional)**
   Vanilla ice cream

In 12-inch skillet, bring I Can't Believe It's Not Butter!® Spread, brown sugar and bananas to a boil. Cook 2 minutes, stirring gently. Carefully add rum to center of pan and cook 15 seconds. Serve hot banana mixture over scoops of ice cream and top, if desired, with sweetened whipped cream.   *Makes 4 servings*

NOTE: Recipe can be halved.

TIP: Choose ripe but firm bananas for this recipe; they will hold their shape better when cooked.

Mom's Pumpkin Pie

Classic Banana Cake

2½ **cups all-purpose flour**

1 **tablespoon baking soda**

½ **teaspoon salt**

1 **cup granulated sugar**

¾ **cup packed light brown sugar**

½ **cup (1 stick) unsalted butter, softened**

2 **eggs**

1 **teaspoon vanilla**

3 **ripe bananas, mashed (about 1⅔ cups)**

⅔ **cup buttermilk**

1 **container (16 ounces) dark chocolate frosting**

1. Preheat oven to 350°F. Grease two 8-inch round cake pans. Combine flour, baking soda and salt in medium bowl.

2. Beat granulated sugar, brown sugar and butter in large bowl with electric mixer at medium speed until light and fluffy. Add eggs and vanilla; beat well. Stir in bananas. Add flour mixture and buttermilk alternately to banana mixture; beat until well blended. Pour batter into prepared pans.

3. Bake about 35 minutes or until toothpick inserted into centers comes out clean. Cool in pans 10 minutes. Remove from pans; cool completely on wire racks.

4. Fill and frost cake with chocolate frosting.   *Makes 12 to 16 servings*

TIP: Make sure the cake layers are completely cool before frosting them. Brush off any loose crumbs from the surfaces. To keep your cake plate clean, place small pieces of waxed paper under the edges of the cake and remove them after the cake has been frosted. For best results, use a flat metal spatula to frost the cake.

Classic Banana Cake

Cinnamon Fruit Crisp

4 medium unpeeled nectarines (about 1½ pounds)

2 large unpeeled plums (about 8 ounces)

5 tablespoons sugar, divided

1½ teaspoons ground cinnamon, divided

¼ cup all-purpose flour

¼ cup uncooked old-fashioned oats

3 tablespoons cold butter, cut into chunks

¼ cup pecan chips, toasted

1. Preheat oven to 375°F.

2. Cut nectarines and plums into slices over medium bowl to catch any juices; discard pits. Add 2 tablespoons sugar and 1 teaspoon cinnamon; mix well. Transfer fruit mixture to 9-inch pie pan.

3. Combine flour, oats, remaining 3 tablespoons sugar and ½ teaspoon cinnamon in small bowl. Cut in butter with pastry blender or two knives until mixture resembles coarse crumbs. Stir in pecans. Sprinkle topping over fruit.

4. Bake 30 minutes or until filling is bubbling, fruit is tender and topping is golden brown. Serve warm or at room temperature. *Makes 6 servings*

White Chocolate Mousse

1 cup vanilla milk chips *or* 7 ounces white chocolate, chopped

¼ cup hot water

2 teaspoons WATKINS® Vanilla

2 cups heavy whipping cream

½ cup sifted powdered sugar

Melt vanilla chips in top of double boiler or in microwave. Add hot water and vanilla; mix until smooth. Cool completely. Beat cream until it begins to thicken. Add sugar; continue beating until soft peaks form. Stir large spoonful of whipped cream into vanilla chip mixture, then fold mixture back into remaining whipped cream. Spoon mousse into individual custard cups or 4-cup mold. Refrigerate until thoroughly chilled. Serve cold. *Makes 8 servings*

Cinnamon Fruit Crisp

Cranberry Pound Cake

1 cup (2 sticks) butter

1½ cups sugar

¼ teaspoon salt

¼ teaspoon ground mace

4 eggs

2 cups cake flour

1 cup chopped fresh or frozen cranberries

1. Preheat oven to 350°F. Grease and flour 9-inch loaf pan.

2. Beat butter, sugar, salt and mace in large bowl with electric mixer at medium speed until light and fluffy. Beat in eggs, 1 at a time, until well blended. Add flour at low speed, ½ cup at a time, scraping down bowl after each addition. Fold in cranberries.

3. Spoon batter into prepared pan. Bake 60 to 70 minutes or until toothpick inserted into center comes out clean. Cool in pan 5 minutes. Run knife around edges to release cake from pan; cool 30 minutes longer. Remove from pan; cool completely on wire rack.

Makes 12 servings

Tip: When fresh or frozen cranberries aren't available, use 1 cup dried sweetened cranberries. Cover cranberries with hot water and let stand 10 minutes. Drain well before using.

Cranberry Pound Cake

Triple Chip Cheesecake

CRUST

1¾ cups chocolate graham cracker crumbs

⅓ cup butter or margarine, melted

FILLING

3 packages (8 ounces *each*) cream cheese, softened

¾ cup granulated sugar

½ cup sour cream

3 tablespoons all-purpose flour

1½ teaspoons vanilla extract

3 large eggs

1 cup (6 ounces) NESTLÉ® TOLL HOUSE® Butterscotch Flavored Morsels

1 cup (6 ounces) NESTLÉ® TOLL HOUSE® Semi-Sweet Chocolate Morsels

1 cup (6 ounces) NESTLÉ® TOLL HOUSE® Premier White Morsels

TOPPING

1 tablespoon *each* NESTLÉ® TOLL HOUSE® Butterscotch Flavored Morsels, Semi-Sweet Chocolate Morsels and Premier White Morsels

PREHEAT oven to 300°F. Grease 9-inch springform pan.

FOR CRUST

COMBINE crumbs and butter in small bowl. Press onto bottom and 1 inch up side of pan.

FOR FILLING

BEAT cream cheese and granulated sugar in large mixer bowl until smooth. Add sour cream, flour and vanilla extract; mix well. Add eggs; beat on low speed until combined.

MELT butterscotch morsels according to package directions. Stir until smooth. Add *1½ cups* batter to melted morsels. Pour into crust. Repeat procedure with semi-sweet morsels. Carefully spoon over butterscotch layer. Melt Premier White morsels according to package directions and blend into *remaining* batter in mixer bowl. Carefully pour over semi-sweet layer.

Continued on page 208

Triple Chip Cheesecake

Triple Chip Cheesecake, continued

BAKE for 1 hour and 10 to 15 minutes or until center is almost set. Cool in pan on wire rack for 10 minutes. Run knife around edge of cheesecake. Let stand for 1 hour.

FOR TOPPING

PLACE each flavor of morsels separately into three small, *heavy-duty* resealable plastic food storage bags. Microwave on HIGH (100%) power for 20 seconds; knead bags to mix. Microwave at additional 10-second intervals, kneading until smooth. Cut small hole in corner of each bag; squeeze to drizzle over cheesecake. Refrigerate for at least 3 hours or overnight. Remove side of pan.   *Makes 12 to 16 servings*

Spicy Applesauce Cake

2¼ **cups all-purpose flour**

  2 **teaspoons baking soda**

  1 **teaspoon ground cinnamon**

  1 **teaspoon ground nutmeg**

 ½ **teaspoon ground cloves**

  1 **cup firmly packed brown sugar**

 ½ **cup FILIPPO BERIO® Olive Oil**

1½ **cups applesauce**

  1 **cup raisins**

  1 **cup coarsely chopped walnuts**

    Powdered sugar or sweetened whipped cream (optional)

Preheat oven to 375°F. Grease 9-inch square pan with olive oil. In medium bowl, combine flour, baking soda, cinnamon, nutmeg and cloves.

In large bowl, mix brown sugar and olive oil with electric mixer at medium speed until blended. Add applesauce; mix well. Add flour mixture all at once; beat at low speed until well blended. Stir in raisins and nuts. Spoon batter into prepared pan.

Bake 20 to 25 minutes or until lightly browned. Cool completely on wire rack. Cut into squares. Serve plain, dusted with powdered sugar or frosted with whipped cream, if desired.

Makes 9 servings

Spicy Applesauce Cake

Double Cherry Crumbles

½ **(18-ounce) package refrigerated oatmeal raisin cookie dough***

½ **cup uncooked old-fashioned oats**

¾ **teaspoon ground cinnamon**

½ **teaspoon ground ginger**

2 **tablespoons cold butter, cut into small pieces**

1 **cup chopped pecans, toasted (see Tip)**

1 **bag (16 ounces) frozen pitted unsweetened dark sweet cherries, thawed**

2 **cans (21 ounces each) cherry pie filling**

Save remaining ½ package of dough for another use.

1. Preheat oven to 350°F. Lightly grease 8 (½-cup) ramekins; place on cookie sheet. Let dough stand at room temperature about 15 minutes.

2. For topping, beat dough, oats, cinnamon and ginger in large bowl until well blended. Cut in butter with pastry blender or 2 knives. Stir in pecans.

3. Combine cherries and pie filling in large bowl; mix well. Divide cherry mixture evenly among prepared ramekins; sprinkle with topping. Bake about 25 minutes or until topping is browned. Serve warm.   *Makes 8 servings*

Tip: To toast pecans, spread them in a single layer on a baking sheet. Bake in a preheated 350°F oven for 7 to 10 minutes or until golden brown, stirring frequently.

Double Cherry Crumbles

Brickle Bundt Cake

1⅓ cups (8-ounce package) HEATH® BITS 'O BRICKLE® Toffee Bits, divided

1¼ cups granulated sugar, divided

¼ cup chopped walnuts

1 teaspoon ground cinnamon

½ cup (1 stick) butter, softened

2 eggs

1¼ teaspoons vanilla extract, divided

2 cups all-purpose flour

1½ teaspoons baking powder

1 teaspoon baking soda

¼ teaspoon salt

1 container (8 ounces) dairy sour cream

¼ cup (½ stick) butter, melted

1 cup powdered sugar

1 to 3 tablespoons milk, divided

1. Heat oven to 325°F. Grease and flour 12-cup fluted tube pan or 10-inch tube pan. Set aside ¼ cup toffee bits for topping. Combine remaining toffee bits, ¼ cup granulated sugar, walnuts and cinnamon; set aside.

2. Beat remaining 1 cup granulated sugar and ½ cup butter in large bowl until fluffy. Add eggs and 1 teaspoon vanilla; beat well. Stir together flour, baking powder, baking soda and salt; gradually add to butter mixture alternately with sour cream, beating until blended. Beat 3 minutes. Spoon one third of batter into prepared pan. Sprinkle with half of toffee mixture. Spoon half of remaining batter into pan. Top with remaining toffee mixture. Spoon remaining batter into pan. Pour melted butter over batter.

3. Bake 45 to 50 minutes or until wooden pick inserted in center comes out clean. Cool 10 minutes; remove from pan to wire rack. Cool completely.

4. Stir together powdered sugar, 1 tablespoon milk and remaining ¼ teaspoon vanilla. Stir in additional milk, 1 teaspoon at a time, until desired consistency; drizzle over cake. Sprinkle with reserved ¼ cup toffee bits.   *Makes 12 to 14 servings*

Brickle Bundt Cake

The Sweet
TABLE

Spiced Raisin Cookies with White Chocolate Drizzle (page 224)

Cranberry Coconut Bars (page 238)

Rocky Road Candy (page 216)

Mocha Fudge Brownies

¾ **cup sugar**

½ **cup (1 stick) butter, softened**

2 **eggs**

3 **squares (1 ounce each) semisweet chocolate, melted**

2 **teaspoons instant espresso powder**

1 **teaspoon vanilla**

½ **cup all-purpose flour**

½ **cup chopped toasted almonds**

1 **cup (6 ounces) milk chocolate chips, divided**

1. Preheat oven to 350°F. Grease 8-inch square baking pan.

2. Beat sugar and butter in medium bowl with electric mixer until well blended. Add eggs; beat until light and fluffy. Add melted chocolate, espresso powder and vanilla; beat until well blended. Stir in flour, almonds and ½ cup chocolate chips. Spread batter evenly in prepared pan.

3. Bake 25 minutes or until firm in center. Remove from oven; sprinkle with remaining ½ cup chocolate chips. Let stand until chips melt; spread evenly over brownies. Cool completely in pan on wire rack. Cut into 2-inch squares.   *Makes 16 brownies*

Rocky Road Candy

2 **cups (12 ounces) semisweet chocolate chips**

2 **tablespoons butter or margarine**

1 **(14-ounce) can EAGLE BRAND® Sweetened Condensed Milk (NOT evaporated milk)**

2 **cups dry-roasted peanuts**

1 **(10½-ounce) package miniature marshmallows**

1. Line 13×9-inch baking pan with wax paper. In heavy saucepan over low heat, melt chocolate chips and butter with EAGLE BRAND®; remove from heat.

2. In large bowl, combine peanuts and marshmallows; stir in chocolate mixture. Spread in prepared pan. Chill 2 hours or until firm.

3. Remove candy from pan; peel off paper and cut into squares. Store loosely covered at room temperature.   *Makes about 3½ dozen candies*

Mocha Fudge Brownies

Lemon Drops

2 cups all-purpose flour

⅛ teaspoon salt

1 cup (2 sticks) butter, softened

1 cup powdered sugar, divided

2 teaspoons lemon juice

1½ teaspoons grated lemon peel (peel of 1 large lemon)

1. Preheat oven to 300°F. Combine flour and salt in medium bowl.

2. Beat butter and ¾ cup powdered sugar in large bowl with electric mixer at medium speed until fluffy. Beat in lemon juice and peel until well blended. Add flour mixture, ½ cup at a time, beating just until blended.

3. Shape dough by rounded teaspoonfuls into balls. Place 1 inch apart on ungreased cookie sheets. Bake 20 to 25 minutes or until just beginning to brown. Cool 5 minutes on cookie sheets. Remove to wire racks; cool completely. Sprinkle with remaining ¼ cup powdered sugar.

Makes about 6 dozen cookies

Classic Layer Bars

1½ cups graham cracker crumbs

½ cup (1 stick) butter, melted

1⅓ cups flaked coconut

1½ cups semisweet chocolate chunks or chips

1 cup chopped nuts

1 can (14 ounces) sweetened condensed milk

1. Preheat oven to 350°F. Combine graham cracker crumbs and butter in medium bowl; press mixture firmly onto bottom of 13×9-inch baking pan.

2. Sprinkle coconut, chocolate chunks and nuts over crumb layer; press down firmly. Pour sweetened condensed milk evenly over top.

3. Bake 25 to 30 minutes or until golden brown. Cool completely on wire rack before cutting into bars.

Makes 3 dozen bars

NOTE: Reduce oven temperature to 325°F if using a glass baking dish.

Lemon Drops

Apricot-Pecan Tassies

  1 cup all-purpose flour

½ cup (1 stick) plus 1 tablespoon butter, cut into pieces, divided

  6 tablespoons cream cheese

¾ cup packed light brown sugar

  1 egg, lightly beaten

½ teaspoon vanilla

¼ teaspoon salt

⅔ cup diced dried apricots

⅓ cup chopped pecans

1. Preheat oven to 325°F. Grease 24 mini (1¾-inch) muffin pan cups or line with paper baking cups.

2. Combine flour, ½ cup butter and cream cheese in food processor. Process using on/off pulses until mixture forms a ball. Wrap dough in plastic wrap; refrigerate 15 minutes.

3. Beat brown sugar, egg, remaining 1 tablespoon butter, vanilla and salt in medium bowl with electric mixer at medium speed until creamy. Stir in apricots and nuts.

4. Shape cold dough into 24 balls. Place each ball in prepared muffin cup; press dough on bottom and up side of each cup. Fill each cup with 1 teaspoon apricot mixture. Bake 25 minutes or until light golden brown. Cool in pans on wire racks.

Makes 2 dozen cookies

Peanut Butter Shortbreads

½ cup (1 stick) unsalted butter, softened

½ cup granulated sugar

¼ cup creamy peanut butter

  2 cups all-purpose flour

Preheat oven to 300°F. Combine all ingredients with fingers in medium bowl until mixture resembles coarse meal. Press into ungreased 8-inch round baking pan. Prick decorative wedges in dough with fork. Bake about 1 hour or until very lightly browned. Cut into wedges while warm.

Makes 16 wedge-shaped cookies

Favorite recipe from **Peanut Advisory Board**

Apricot-Pecan Tassies

Chocolate Buttercream Cherry Candies

About 48 maraschino cherries with stems, well drained

2 cups powdered sugar

¼ cup (½ stick) butter, softened

¼ cup HERSHEY'S Cocoa or HERSHEY'S SPECIAL DARK™ Cocoa

1 to 2 tablespoons milk, divided

½ teaspoon vanilla extract

¼ teaspoon almond extract

White Chip Coating (recipe follows)

Chocolate Chip Drizzle (recipe follows)

1. Cover tray with wax paper. Lightly press cherries between layers of paper towels to remove excess moisture.

2. Beat powdered sugar, butter, cocoa and 1 tablespoon milk in small bowl until well blended; stir in vanilla and almond extract. If necessary, add remaining milk, one teaspoon at a time, until mixture will hold together but is not wet.

3. Mold scant teaspoon mixture around each cherry, covering completely; place on prepared tray. Cover; refrigerate 3 hours or until firm.

4. Prepare White Chip Coating. Holding each cherry by stem, dip into coating. Place on tray; refrigerate until firm.

5. About 1 hour before serving, prepare Chocolate Chip Drizzle; with tines of fork, drizzle randomly over candies. Refrigerate until drizzle is firm. Store in refrigerator.

Makes about 48 candies

WHITE CHIP COATING: Place 2 cups (12-ounce package) HERSHEY'S Premier White Chips in small microwave-safe bowl; drizzle with 2 tablespoons vegetable oil. Microwave at HIGH (100%) 1 minute; stir. If necessary, microwave at HIGH an additional 15 seconds at a time, stirring after each heating just until chips are melted and mixture is smooth. If mixture thickens while coating, microwave at HIGH 15 seconds; stir until smooth.

CHOCOLATE CHIP DRIZZLE: Place ¼ cup HERSHEY'S Semi-Sweet Chocolate Chips and ¼ teaspoon shortening (do not use butter, margarine, spread or oil) in another small microwave-safe bowl. Microwave at HIGH (100%) 30 seconds to 1 minute; stir until chips are melted and mixture is smooth.

Chocolate Buttercream Cherry Candies

Spiced Raisin Cookies with White Chocolate Drizzle

2 cups all-purpose flour
1½ teaspoons ground cinnamon
1 teaspoon baking soda
1 teaspoon ground ginger
½ teaspoon ground allspice
¼ teaspoon salt
1 cup sugar
¾ cup butter, softened
¼ cup molasses
1 egg
1 cup SUN-MAID® Raisins or Golden Raisins
4 ounces white chocolate, coarsely chopped

HEAT oven to 375°F.

COMBINE flour, cinnamon, baking soda, ginger, allspice and salt in small bowl. Set aside.

BEAT sugar and butter until light and fluffy. Add molasses and egg; beat well.

BEAT in raisins. Gradually beat in flour mixture on low speed just until incorporated.

DROP dough by tablespoonfuls onto ungreased cookie sheets 2 inches apart. Flatten dough slightly.

BAKE 12 to 14 minutes or until set. Cool on cookie sheets 1 minute; transfer to wire racks and cool completely.

MICROWAVE chocolate in heavy, resealable plastic bag at high power 30 seconds. Turn bag over; heat additional 30 to 45 seconds or until almost melted. Knead bag with hands to melt remaining chocolate. Cut ⅛-inch corner off one end of bag. Drizzle cooled cookies with chocolate. Let stand until chocolate is set, about 20 minutes.

Makes about 2 dozen cookies

Prep Time: 15 minutes
Bake Time: 14 minutes

Spiced Raisin Cookies with White Chocolate Drizzle

Coconut Brownie Bites

42 MOUNDS® or ALMOND JOY® Candy Bar Miniatures

½ **cup (1 stick) butter or margarine, softened**

½ **cup packed light brown sugar**

¼ **cup granulated sugar**

1 **egg**

1 **teaspoon vanilla extract**

1¼ **cups all-purpose flour**

⅓ **cup HERSHEY'S Cocoa**

¾ **teaspoon baking soda**

½ **teaspoon salt**

1. Remove wrappers from candies. Line small muffin cups (1¾ inches in diameter) with paper baking cups.

2. Beat butter, brown sugar, granulated sugar, egg and vanilla in large bowl until well blended. Stir together flour, cocoa, baking soda and salt; gradually add to butter mixture, beating until well blended. Cover; refrigerate dough about 30 minutes or until firm enough to handle.

3. Heat oven to 375°F. Shape dough into 1-inch balls; place one ball in each prepared muffin cup. *Do not flatten.*

4. Bake 8 to 10 minutes or until puffed. Remove from oven. Cool 5 minutes. (Cookies will sink slightly.) Press one candy onto each cookie. Cool completely in pan on wire racks.

Makes 3½ dozen cookies

Coconut Brownie Bites

Lemon-Up Cakes

1 package (about 18 ounces) butter recipe white cake mix with pudding in the mix, plus ingredients to prepare mix

½ cup fresh lemon juice, divided (2 large lemons)

Grated peel of 2 lemons, divided

½ cup (1 stick) butter, softened

3½ cups powdered sugar

Yellow food coloring

1 package (9½ ounces) lemon-shaped hard candies, coarsely crushed

1. Preheat oven to 350°F. Line 24 standard (2½-inch) muffin pan cups with paper baking cups.

2. Prepare cake mix according to package directions but use ¼ cup less water than called for in directions. Stir in ¼ cup lemon juice and half of grated lemon peel. Fill muffin cups evenly with batter.

3. Bake 23 minutes or until light golden brown and toothpick inserted into centers comes out clean. Cool cupcakes in pans on wire racks 5 minutes. Remove from pans; cool completely on wire racks.

4. Beat butter in large bowl with electric mixer at medium speed until creamy. Gradually add powdered sugar until blended. Add remaining ¼ cup lemon juice, remaining half of lemon peel and several drops food coloring; beat at high speed until frosting is light and fluffy.

5. Frost cupcakes. Sprinkle crushed candies over frosting.   *Makes 2 dozen cupcakes*

Tip: If your frosting is too stiff to spread easily, beat in additional lemon juice or milk, one teaspoon at a time, until the desired consistency is reached. If the frosting is soft because too much liquid was used, beat in some additional sifted powdered sugar.

Lemon-Up Cakes

Pumpkin Pie Bars

1½ **cups plus 1 tablespoon all-purpose flour, divided**

1 **cup finely chopped nuts**

½ **cup granulated sugar**

½ **cup firmly packed brown sugar**

2 **teaspoons ground cinnamon, divided**

¾ **cup (1½ sticks) butter or margarine**

1 **(15-ounce) can pumpkin (2 cups)**

1 **(14-ounce) can EAGLE BRAND® Sweetened Condensed Milk (NOT evaporated milk)**

2 **eggs, beaten**

½ **teaspoon ground allspice**

¼ **teaspoon salt**

1. Preheat oven to 375°F. In medium bowl, combine 1½ cups flour, nuts, granulated sugar, brown sugar and 1 teaspoon cinnamon. Add butter; mix until crumbly. Reserve 1¼ cups flour mixture. Pat remaining mixture on bottom of ungreased 13×9-inch baking pan.

2. In large bowl, combine pumpkin, EAGLE BRAND®, eggs, remaining 1 teaspoon cinnamon, allspice and salt; mix well. Pour evenly over crust.

3. Mix reserved flour mixture with remaining 1 tablespoon flour. Sprinkle over pumpkin mixture. Bake 30 to 35 minutes or until set. Cool 10 minutes. Serve warm. Store leftovers covered in refrigerator.   *Makes 2 dozen bars*

Prep Time: 15 minutes

Pumpkin Pie Bars

Reese's® Double Peanut Butter and Milk Chocolate Chip Cookies

¾ **cup sugar**

½ **cup (1 stick) butter or margarine, softened**

⅓ **cup REESE'S® Creamy or Crunchy Peanut Butter**

1 **egg**

½ **teaspoon vanilla extract**

1¼ **cups all-purpose flour**

½ **teaspoon baking soda**

¼ **teaspoon salt**

1 **cup HERSHEY₅S Milk Chocolate Chips**

1 **cup REESE'S® Peanut Butter Chips**

1. Heat oven to 350°F.

2. Beat sugar, butter and peanut butter in medium bowl until creamy. Add egg and vanilla; beat well. Stir together flour, baking soda and salt; add to butter mixture, blending well. Stir in milk chocolate chips and peanut butter chips. Drop by rounded teaspoons onto ungreased cookie sheets.

3. Bake 12 to 14 minutes or until light golden brown around edges. Cool 1 minute on cookie sheets. Remove to wire racks; cool completely. *Makes about 3 dozen cookies*

Reese's® Double Peanut Butter and Milk Chocolate Chip Cookies

Intense Mint-Chocolate Brownies

BROWNIES

1 cup (2 sticks) butter

4 squares (1 ounce each) unsweetened chocolate

1½ cups granulated sugar

3 eggs

½ teaspoon salt

½ teaspoon mint extract

½ teaspoon vanilla

¾ cup all-purpose flour

MINT FROSTING

6 tablespoons butter, softened

1 teaspoon mint extract

2 to 3 drops green food coloring

2 cups powdered sugar

2 to 3 tablespoons milk

CHOCOLATE GLAZE

⅓ cup semisweet chocolate chips

2 tablespoons butter

1. Preheat oven to 325°F. Grease and flour 9-inch square baking pan.

2. For brownies, melt butter and chocolate in top of double boiler over simmering water. Remove from heat. Beat in granulated sugar, eggs, salt, mint extract and vanilla until well blended. Stir in flour. Spread batter in prepared pan. Bake 35 minutes or until top is firm and edges begin to pull away from sides of pan. Cool completely in pan on wire rack.

3. For frosting, beat butter, mint extract and food coloring in large bowl with electric mixer at medium speed until fluffy. Gradually add powdered sugar. Beat in milk, 1 tablespoon at a time, until frosting is of spreading consistency. Spread frosting over cooled brownies.

4. For glaze, place chocolate chips and butter in microwavable bowl. Microwave on LOW (30%) 1 minute; stir. Repeat until chocolate is melted and mixture is smooth. Drizzle glaze over frosting. Let stand 30 minutes or until glaze is set.   *Makes 2 dozen brownies*

Intense Mint-Chocolate Brownies

Chocolate Coconut Mini Cheesecakes

   1 cup chocolate cookie crumbs

   ¼ cup (½ stick) butter or margarine, melted

   2 packages (8 ounces each) cream cheese, softened

   ⅓ cup sugar

   2 eggs

   1 teaspoon vanilla

   ¼ teaspoon coconut extract (optional)

   ½ cup flaked coconut

   ½ cup semisweet chocolate chips

   1 teaspoon shortening

1. Preheat oven to 325°F. Line 12 standard (2½-inch) muffin pan cups with foil or paper baking cups.

2. Combine cookie crumbs and butter in small bowl. Press onto bottoms of prepared muffin cups.

3. Combine cream cheese and sugar in large bowl; beat with electric mixer at medium speed 2 minutes or until well blended. Add eggs, vanilla and coconut extract, if desired; beat just until blended. Stir in flaked coconut.

4. Carefully spoon about ¼ cup cream cheese mixture into each baking cup. Bake 18 to 22 minutes or until nearly set. Cool 30 minutes in pan on wire rack. Remove from pan; peel off baking cups.

5. Melt chocolate chips and shortening in small saucepan over low heat, stirring frequently, until chocolate is melted. Drizzle over cheesecakes. Let stand 20 minutes. Refrigerate until ready to serve.   *Makes 12 servings*

Chocolate Coconut Mini Cheesecakes

Cranberry Coconut Bars

FILLING

2 cups fresh or thawed frozen cranberries

1 cup dried sweetened cranberries

⅔ cup granulated sugar

¼ cup water

Grated peel of 1 lemon

CRUST

1¼ cups all-purpose flour

¾ cup uncooked old-fashioned oats

½ teaspoon baking soda

½ teaspoon salt

1 cup firmly packed light brown sugar

¾ cup (1½ sticks) butter, softened

1 cup shredded sweetened coconut

1 cup chopped toasted pecans*

To toast pecans, spread in single layer on baking sheet. Bake in preheated 350°F oven 5 to 7 minutes or until golden brown, stirring frequently.

1. Preheat oven to 400°F. Grease and flour 13×9-inch baking pan.

2. For filling, combine fresh cranberries, dried cranberries, granulated sugar, water and lemon peel in medium saucepan. Cook 10 to 15 minutes over medium-high heat until mixture is pulpy, stirring frequently. Mash cranberries with back of spoon. Cool to lukewarm.

3. For crust, combine flour, oats, baking soda and salt in medium bowl. Beat brown sugar and butter in large bowl with electric mixer at medium speed until creamy. Add flour mixture; beat just until blended. Stir in coconut and pecans. Reserve 1½ cups; pat remaining crumb mixture onto bottom of prepared pan. Bake 10 minutes; remove from oven.

4. Gently spread cranberry filling over crust. Sprinkle with reserved crumb mixture. Bake 18 to 20 minutes or until bars are set and crust is golden brown. Cool completely before cutting into bars. *Makes 2 dozen bars*

Cranberry Coconut Bars

Milk Chocolate Florentine Cookies

⅔ **cup butter**

2 **cups quick oats**

1 **cup granulated sugar**

⅔ **cup all-purpose flour**

¼ **cup light or dark corn syrup**

¼ **cup milk**

1 **teaspoon vanilla extract**

¼ **teaspoon salt**

1¾ **cups (11.5-ounce package) NESTLÉ® TOLL HOUSE® Milk Chocolate Morsels**

PREHEAT oven to 375°F. Line baking sheets with foil.

MELT butter in medium saucepan; remove from heat. Stir in oats, sugar, flour, corn syrup, milk, vanilla extract and salt; mix well. Drop by level teaspoon, about 3 inches apart, onto prepared baking sheets. Spread thinly with rubber spatula.

BAKE for 6 to 8 minutes or until golden brown. Cool completely on baking sheets on wire racks. Peel foil from cookies.

MICROWAVE morsels in medium, uncovered, microwave-safe bowl on MEDIUM-HIGH (70%) power for 1 minute. Stir. Morsels may retain some of their original shape. If necessary, microwave at additional 10- to 15-second intervals, stirring just until morsels are melted. Spread thin layer of melted chocolate onto flat side of *half* the cookies. Top with *remaining* cookies. *Makes about 3½ dozen sandwich cookies*

Milk Chocolate Florentine Cookies

Toffee Studded Snickerdoodles

½ **cup (1 stick) butter or margarine, softened**

½ **cup shortening**

1 **cup plus 3 tablespoons sugar, divided**

2 **eggs**

2¾ **cups all-purpose flour**

2 **teaspoons cream of tartar**

1 **teaspoon baking soda**

¼ **teaspoon salt**

1⅓ **cups (8-ounce package) HEATH® BITS 'O BRICKLE® Toffee Bits**

1 **teaspoon ground cinnamon**

1. Heat oven to 400°F.

2. Beat butter, shortening and 1 cup sugar in large bowl until fluffy. Add eggs; beat thoroughly. Stir together flour, cream of tartar, baking soda and salt; gradually add to butter mixture, beating until well blended. Stir in toffee bits.

3. Stir together remaining 3 tablespoons sugar and cinnamon. Shape dough into 1¼-inch balls; roll in sugar-cinnamon mixture. Place on ungreased cookie sheets.

4. Bake 9 to 11 minutes or until lightly browned around edges. Cool 1 minute; remove from cookie sheets to wire racks. Cool completely. *Makes about 5 dozen cookies*

Tip: When cooling cookies, arrange them in a single layer on a wire rack; do not overlap them or they will become soggy.

Toffee Studded Snickerdoodles

Sensational Cinnamon Chip Biscotti

  1 cup sugar

  ½ cup (1 stick) butter, softened

  2 eggs

  1 teaspoon vanilla extract

2½ cups all-purpose flour

1½ teaspoons baking powder

  ¼ teaspoon salt

1⅔ cups (10-ounce package) HERSHEY⚬S Cinnamon Chips, divided

  1 cup very finely chopped walnuts

  2 teaspoons shortening (do not use butter, margarine, spread or oil)

    White Chip Drizzle (recipe follows)

1. Heat oven to 325°F. Lightly grease cookie sheets.

2. Beat sugar and butter in large bowl until blended. Add eggs and vanilla; beat well. Stir together flour, baking powder and salt; gradually add to butter mixture, beating until smooth. (Dough will be stiff.) Using spoon or with hands, work 1 cup cinnamon chips and walnuts into dough.

3. Divide dough into four equal parts. Shape each part into log about 8 inches long. Place on prepared cookie sheets at least 2 inches apart; flatten slightly.

4. Bake 25 to 30 minutes or until logs are set and wooden pick inserted into centers comes out clean. Remove from oven; let cool on cookie sheets 30 minutes. Transfer to cutting board. Using serrated knife and sawing motion, cut logs diagonally into ½-inch-wide slices. Place slices close together, cut side down, on ungreased cookie sheets. Return to oven; bake 5 to 6 minutes. Turn each slice; bake an additional 5 to 8 minutes. Remove from oven; cool slightly. Remove from cookie sheets to wire racks; cool completely. Melt remaining cinnamon chips with shortening; drizzle over each cookie. Drizzle White Chip Drizzle over top.   *Makes about 5 dozen cookies*

WHITE CHIP DRIZZLE: Place ¼ cup HERSHEY⚬S Premier White Chips and 1 teaspoon shortening (do not use butter, margarine, spread or oil) in small microwave-safe bowl. Microwave at HIGH (100%) 30 to 45 seconds or until smooth when stirred.

Sensational Cinnamon Chip Biscotti

Two-Tone Cheesecake Bars

2 cups finely crushed creme-filled chocolate sandwich cookie crumbs (about 24 cookies)

3 tablespoons butter or margarine, melted

3 (8-ounce) packages cream cheese, softened

1 (14-ounce) can EAGLE BRAND® Sweetened Condensed Milk (NOT evaporated milk)

3 eggs

2 teaspoons vanilla extract

2 (1-ounce) squares unsweetened chocolate, melted

Chocolate Glaze (recipe follows)

1. Preheat oven to 300°F. In medium bowl, combine cookie crumbs and butter; press firmly onto bottom of ungreased 13×9-inch baking pan.

2. In large bowl, beat cream cheese until fluffy. Gradually beat in EAGLE BRAND® until smooth. Add eggs and vanilla; mix well. Pour half of batter evenly over prepared crust. Stir melted chocolate into remaining batter; pour evenly over plain batter.

3. Bake 55 to 60 minutes or until set. Cool. Top with Chocolate Glaze. Chill. Cut into bars. Store leftovers covered in refrigerator.   *Makes 2 to 3 dozen bars*

Chocolate Glaze

2 (1-ounce) squares unsweetened chocolate

2 tablespoons butter or margarine

Pinch salt

1¾ cups powdered sugar

3 tablespoons hot water or cream

In heavy saucepan over low heat, melt chocolate and butter with salt. Remove from heat. Add powdered sugar and hot water; mix well. Immediately spread over bars.

Makes about 1 cup glaze

Acknowledgments

The publisher would like to thank the companies and organizations listed below for the use of their recipes and photographs in this publication.

ACH Food Companies, Inc.

Allen Canning Company

American Lamb Council

Bob Evans®

Cabot® Creamery Cooperative

Del Monte Corporation

Dole Food Company, Inc.

EAGLE BRAND®

Filippo Berio® Olive Oil

The Hershey Company

The Hidden Valley® Food Products Company

Hillshire Farm®

Hormel Foods, LLC

Jennie-O Turkey Store®

MASTERFOODS USA

McIlhenny Company (TABASCO® brand Pepper Sauce)

Mrs. Dash®

National Cattlemen's Beef Association on Behalf of The Beef Checkoff

National Honey Board

National Pork Board

Nestlé USA

New York Apple Association, Inc.

Ortega®, A Division of B&G Foods, Inc.

Peanut Advisory Board

The Quaker® Oatmeal Kitchens

Reckitt Benckiser Inc.

Reprinted with permission of Sunkist Growers, Inc. All Rights Reserved.

Sun•Maid® Growers of California

Unilever

U.S. Highbush Blueberry Council

USA Rice Federation™

Watkins Incorporated

Wisconsin Milk Marketing Board

Debbie Mumm blends nostalgia, humor, and a bit of whimsy into every design she creates. Her delightfully detailed artwork can be found on many charming products.

METRIC CONVERSION CHART

VOLUME MEASUREMENTS (dry)

1/8 teaspoon = 0.5 mL
1/4 teaspoon = 1 mL
1/2 teaspoon = 2 mL
3/4 teaspoon = 4 mL
1 teaspoon = 5 mL
1 tablespoon = 15 mL
2 tablespoons = 30 mL
1/4 cup = 60 mL
1/3 cup = 75 mL
1/2 cup = 125 mL
2/3 cup = 150 mL
3/4 cup = 175 mL
1 cup = 250 mL
2 cups = 1 pint = 500 mL
3 cups = 750 mL
4 cups = 1 quart = 1 L

VOLUME MEASUREMENTS (fluid)

1 fluid ounce (2 tablespoons) = 30 mL
4 fluid ounces (1/2 cup) = 125 mL
8 fluid ounces (1 cup) = 250 mL
12 fluid ounces (1 1/2 cups) = 375 mL
16 fluid ounces (2 cups) = 500 mL

WEIGHTS (mass)

1/2 ounce = 15 g
1 ounce = 30 g
3 ounces = 90 g
4 ounces = 120 g
8 ounces = 225 g
10 ounces = 285 g
12 ounces = 360 g
16 ounces = 1 pound = 450 g

DIMENSIONS

1/16 inch = 2 mm
1/8 inch = 3 mm
1/4 inch = 6 mm
1/2 inch = 1.5 cm
3/4 inch = 2 cm
1 inch = 2.5 cm

OVEN TEMPERATURES

250°F = 120°C
275°F = 140°C
300°F = 150°C
325°F = 160°C
350°F = 180°C
375°F = 190°C
400°F = 200°C
425°F = 220°C
450°F = 230°C

BAKING PAN SIZES

Utensil	Size in Inches/Quarts	Metric Volume	Size in Centimeters
Baking or	8 × 8 × 2	2 L	20 × 20 × 5
Cake Pan	9 × 9 × 2	2.5 L	23 × 23 × 5
(square or	12 × 8 × 2	3 L	30 × 20 × 5
rectangular)	13 × 9 × 2	3.5 L	33 × 23 × 5
Loaf Pan	8 × 4 × 3	1.5 L	20 × 10 × 7
	9 × 5 × 3	2 L	23 × 13 × 7
Round Layer	8 × 1½	1.2 L	20 × 4
Cake Pan	9 × 1½	1.5 L	23 × 4
Pie Plate	8 × 1¼	750 mL	20 × 3
	9 × 1¼	1 L	23 × 3
Baking Dish	1 quart	1 L	—
or Casserole	1½ quart	1.5 L	—
	2 quart	2 L	—